Copyright © 2024 by Derrick Solano
All rights reserved. No part of this book may be reproduced in any manner whatsoever without written permission except in the case of brief quotations embodied in critical articles and reviews.
First Printing, 2024

I WON'T BREAK

I WON'T BREAK

DERRICK SOLANO

CONTENTS

Dedication   ix

Prologue: The Moment I Lost Everything   1

1   Two Years Old and Forgotten   5

2   Ghosts of the Foster System   9

3   The Last Home Before We Were Split   13

4   Stripped of Safety   17

5   A Name Without a Family   21

6   Humiliation as Control   25

7   Back in Morenci   29

8   A Dark Turn in High School   33

9   Young, Wild, and Scared   37

10   The Beginning of the End   41

11   An Impossible Fight   45

12   The End of Us   47

13   Brother in Chaos   51

14   Running and Escaping   55

15   Caught in the Web   59

16   Breaking Point   63

17	The ICU and the Second Fall	67
18	Running from Everything	71
19	Waves of Freedom and Chains of Betrayal	75
20	Returning to Familiar Chaos	79
21	Spiraling and New Beginnings	83
22	A Love Built in Chaos	87
23	A Toxic Love in the Desert	91
24	Death, Grief, and a Golden UFO	95
25	Success, Strain, and the Return of My Sister	99
26	A Betrayal, a Goodbye, and a New Beginning	103
27	A New Home, A New Life	107
28	The Shadows of the Past	111
29	One Dollar Over a Hundred Pennies	115
30	A Future Built on Truth	119
	Final Reflections: Sink or Swim	123

About the Author   124

To Caleb,
You were taken from me, but you've never left my heart. No matter where life takes us, know that I've always loved you, and I always will.

To Anthony,
My rock, my love, my lifeline. Through every storm, you've stood by my side. I wouldn't be here without you.

To Blanca,
For always staying by my side, reminding me that even in the darkest moments, there's still a light worth holding onto.

And to anyone who's ever felt broken, abandoned, or lost—this is for you. You are not alone. We rise, we fight, and we survive. We won't break.

Prologue: The Moment I Lost Everything

I was 24 years old, sitting in a cold Texas jail cell, waiting to be transferred back to Arizona. Back to the life I had tried so fucking hard to run away from. It was a long way from where I'd been just a few years earlier, but maybe that's why it hurt so much. Everything I had tried to escape, every piece of trauma I'd buried, every broken part of my past—it had all caught up to me.

I'd already lost Caleb by then. He was taken from me when I was 22. That was the first time I felt the cracks, but it wasn't enough to break me yet. I was still trying to fight, trying to hold on to something, even if it was just the lie that I could make things better.

But by the time I ended up in that jail, I wasn't fighting anymore. I had nothing left. I'd been on probation for a felony—identity theft. I used someone else's credit to get furniture from Ashley Furniture, trying to piece together a life with Hope, even though everything was already falling apart by then. That was after Caleb had already been taken, after I had tried to overdose on pills to escape the pain. After I'd landed in the ICU, hooked up to machines, having to learn how to walk again.

Teresa came to see me in the hospital. I remember the look on her face. She didn't come to offer comfort or love—she came to watch me die. I'm sure of it. And when I didn't die, when I came out of that hell, I realized something. I couldn't stay. I couldn't do this anymore.

So I packed up my shit and left. I ran to Galveston, Texas, hiding from my probation, hiding from everything. I thought I could escape. I thought I could outrun all the pain, all the trauma, all the guilt. But the thing about running is that you can only go so far before the weight of it all drags you down.

And it did.

Two years later, they caught up with me. I was thrown into that Texas jail, waiting to be shipped back to Arizona, back to Safford, back to the life I had tried so hard to leave behind. I had no one. I wrote to my adoptive parents, tried calling them. Nothing. They didn't give a shit. They didn't want anything to do with me. I realized in that cell that if I died, no one would know. No one would care.

That's when it hit me. That's when I first realized I had lost everything.

I had no one. Not a single soul on this fucking planet cared whether I lived or died. And in that moment, as I sat in that cell, it all came crashing down. The trauma I'd been carrying since I was a kid, the years of not being good enough, the secrets I'd been forced to keep—it all led me here. Sitting in a jail cell, broken and alone, realizing that I had been running from myself for so long that I didn't even know who I was anymore.

This was my rock bottom. This was the moment I knew.

I tried reaching out to them—my adoptive parents. Even after everything, after all the abuse, the lies, and the manipulation, I still tried. Maybe part of me believed that somewhere inside them, they cared. That they would see me in that jail cell, realize I was broken, and offer some kind of fucking help. But that's not what happened.

I started with phone calls. I sat in that cold, empty cell, waiting for them to pick up, hoping they'd at least hear me out. But they didn't. They wouldn't even take the call from the jail. The line would go dead, and I'd be left there, the phone heavy in my hand, knowing that on the other side was silence. It wasn't anything new for me—heartbreak had been my companion for as long as I could remember. But it doesn't get easier. It just gets more familiar, like an old wound that never fully heals.

And so, I turned to writing. I started sending letters from that jail. I wasn't expecting miracles, but I was hoping for... something. Some kind of acknowledgment. Maybe even just a scrap of love, or at least a mention of Caleb. But the few times they responded, it was nothing but "I told you so." They had always told me I'd end up like this, and here I was, proving them right.

It wasn't love. It wasn't even concern. It was just more judgment, more condemnation. And not once did they mention Caleb. Not once. They weren't going to.

They weren't going to talk about him because they didn't want me to think I could ever be part of his life again. They didn't want me thinking that once I got out of jail, I could come for him, try to reclaim him. They had replaced me, and now Caleb was *their* son. In their eyes, I was nothing. I didn't exist anymore.

That silence about Caleb was more than cruel—it was a message. A reminder that I had been erased from his life, that I no longer had any claim to being his father. He was theirs now, and there was no room for me in that picture. My role in their lives, in his life, was over.

That hit harder than anything else. They didn't even need to say it out loud. Their silence said it all: I was gone, forgotten, replaced. Caleb was theirs, and I was nothing.

That silence, that refusal to acknowledge him, made it feel like I had lost him completely. It wasn't just that he was physically taken from me—it was that they had erased my right to even think of myself as his dad. Whatever small part of me that still believed I could be his father, that I still mattered in his life, was crushed under the weight of that silence.

They had finally won. And I had nothing.

But I knew I couldn't let it eat me alive. I had to make the best of it. If I didn't, I'd never make it out. I cried at night, sure—hugging myself, trying to keep the weight of everything from crushing me—but during the day, I focused on anything else. I wrote. I drew. I made plans for the future, even if those plans seemed impossible. My imagination became my escape, the only thing I could hold onto when everything else had been stripped away.

I couldn't control what was happening in the real world, but I could still control what was in my hands. No one could take that away from me. Not Terry and Teresa. Not the jail. Not the system that had abandoned me long ago.

There isn't any one song or piece of writing that stands out from that time. It's all gone now, thrown away when I left jail, lost to the same void that had swallowed up so much of my life. But what I remember is the relief I found in creating them. It was the process that mattered, not the result. The act of creating gave me something that the world couldn't take away—something that was mine.

And that's what kept me going. Even when everything else was falling apart, I still had that. I might have lost Caleb, I might have lost my family, but I hadn't lost *me*. As long as I could write, as long as I could dream, there was still a part of me that refused to break.

CHAPTER 1

Two Years Old and Forgotten

The earliest memory I have is like a dream, but I know it was real. I can still see the small apartment, the walls stained with smoke, the air heavy with the smell of cigarettes and cheap beer. There were people everywhere, talking loud, laughing too hard. They passed me around like some kind of party favor, getting me to take sips of alcohol even though I was just a baby, not even two years old. That's who they were. That's who *he* was—my biological father, throwing a party while I watched everything unravel around me.

I remember something else from that night, too. Something that still makes my skin crawl when I think about it. They tried to circumcise me. I was just a kid, sitting there, and someone pulled out a pair of scissors. They didn't go through with it, but that image, that memory, is seared into my brain. That was my introduction to the world. That's what family looked like to me before I even knew what the word meant.

But it wasn't the party, the drinking, or the scissors that truly broke me. That came later.

I was two years old, just a kid, too young to understand what was happening, but old enough to feel it in my bones. I can still see her—my biological mother, her long curly brown hair falling over her shoulders as she held my hand in one of hers and a blue cake in the other. We were walking down the hallway at the DES office, and to her, it felt like a celebration. Like this was a good thing. Like handing me over to strangers, abandoning me, was something to be proud of.

That was the last time I ever saw her. That was the last time I ever heard from her.

She gave me up that day, and with her went any chance I ever had of understanding what family was supposed to be. I don't know if she cried later, if she regretted it, or if she walked out of that office without looking back. But I do know that in that moment, something inside me broke. Something that could have been love, that could have been trust, that could have allowed me to connect with people later in life—it all shattered right there, in that hallway, with the blue cake and her hand slipping out of mine.

I've never been able to attach to people after that. Not really. I've seen people with families, seen them laugh and hold each other close, but it's always been like looking through a window from the outside. I've never been able to understand that connection. How could I, when the first thing I learned about family was that it could be taken away in a heartbeat?

But that's not the only memory I have from those early days. There's another one, more like a nightmare. It's my mom, the same woman who gave me up, being thrown around our small apartment by my dad. I can still see it happening—her body hitting the walls, the screams, the chaos. My brother John, my sister Tasha, and I had to hide down the hall, trying to disappear into the shadows while everything fell apart in the next room.

After that, our mom disappeared for days. We didn't know where she went, and we didn't have anyone to take care of us. There was no electricity in the apartment, no food except for a pot of dried-up macaroni and cheese on the stove and a jar of peanut butter. We were left there, three kids in the dark, alone. John was four. Tasha was three. I had barely turned two.

That's the last thing I remember from those days. Everything else is a blur, like my mind decided it was better to forget. Maybe it was. Maybe remembering any more would have been too much to carry. But even though I don't remember it all, the damage was already done. By the time I was handed over to the state, I was already broken.

I didn't know it then, but that day—walking down that hallway, watching my mother disappear from my life—was the beginning of everything. It set the tone for the rest of my life. Abandonment. Rejection. Being handed over, left behind. That's what family meant to me. And no matter what happened after, I could never shake the feeling that I was always going to be the kid no one wanted. The kid who wasn't enough.

CHAPTER 2

Ghosts of the Foster System

One of the first foster homes I remember was with a family named Lynn and Billy Pace. I don't know how long we were with them—time is a blur when you're a kid and everything around you feels like chaos—but I know it was a couple of years. Long enough to leave scars. They had a daughter, Windy. She was older than the three of us—me, John, and Tasha—and she had a deformed hand from an accident. I remember feeling sorry for her, even then, because no one in that house was safe from the abuse. Not even her.

The Paces were the kind of people who made you believe that things might be okay for a little while, only to pull the rug out from under you when you least expected it. Lynn was kind sometimes, giving us chalk to draw on the sidewalk, buying us toys, even giving me a baby horse. There were children's books, moments where I almost believed that maybe this place would be different. But then Billy would come home, and everything would change.

I remember one day vividly. Tasha and I were drawing on the sidewalk with the chalk Lynn had given us. It was one of those moments where everything felt normal, almost peaceful, like we could just be kids. But that didn't last. Billy came home from work, and he was mad—probably drunk. His anger came out of nowhere, like a storm building up behind the clouds, and before I knew what was happening, he punched me in the head. Full force.

Everything went black after that.

When I woke up, I was in bed. Hours had passed, and Lynn was sitting beside me, blowing on me like a fan, too scared to take me to the hospital. I don't know if it was fear of what people would say, or fear of Billy himself, but she didn't want anyone to know. I didn't matter enough to be protected, to be taken care of. I was just another burden.

That house was full of those moments. Billy's anger. Lynn's fear. Windy's silent suffering. It was like we were all trapped, forced to act like adults, even though we were just kids. And when I finally came out about the abuse, we were removed from that home. That's what it took—me speaking up, even though I didn't want to, even though I was terrified. But I couldn't take it anymore. None of us could.

Leaving that home should have felt like freedom, but it didn't. We were taken to daycare while they arranged for us to be moved. Lynn usually showed up to pick us up riding a horse because the daycare was just down the street from where they lived. But that day, she came in a car. It was different, and even as a kid, I knew something wasn't right.

She put all three of us in the car—me, John, and Tasha—and drove a little way down the road before pulling over. She turned to us, tears in her eyes, and told us that we were leaving. That we wouldn't be coming back. And then she said something that broke my heart in a way I didn't even understand at the time: *"I wish I could be your mommy forever."*

We were kids, and we didn't know what to do with that. We cried. We begged her to let us stay, but there was nothing she could do. Or at least, that's what she said. Looking back, I don't know what was real and what wasn't in that moment. All I know is that it shattered me, and I was left once again feeling like I didn't belong anywhere.

That was one of the last homes we were in together before we were separated. After that, John, Tasha, and I were split up, sent to different homes, different lives. But I didn't know that was coming yet. I was just a kid, holding onto whatever I could to feel safe. When we were moved, I was given a little white stuffed dog by DES, a small comfort in the middle of so much confusion and pain.

That dog became my best friend. I held it when I cried. I talked to it like it was the only one who understood me. And in some ways, it was. That little stuffed dog was my whole world in those moments. Even though I lost it eventually, I never forgot the way it made me feel—safe, even when everything around me was crumbling.

All these years later, I still think about that little white dog. Out of all my eight dogs today, the one closest to me, the one who never leaves my side, is Blanca. She's pure white, just like that stuffed dog was. I like to think of her as my spirit animal, the one who's always with me, keeping me grounded. She's a reminder that even in the darkest times, there's something worth holding onto. Something that makes you feel less alone, even if it's just a memory of a stuffed animal you lost years ago.

CHAPTER 3

The Last Home Before We Were Split

After we left Lynn and Billy's house, we ended up in another foster home, but this one didn't seem like anything out of the ordinary at first. I was too young to understand the twisted irony that would only reveal itself to me in adulthood. The fucked-up part? This home wasn't just another stop in the foster system—it belonged to my adoptive parents' distant cousins.

Their names were Danny and Vicky Richins, and we were placed with them in Duncan, Arizona. I had no idea then, of course, that I would eventually end up with another pair of Richins. It was just another house in a line of houses that we were shuffled through, but the memories from that place still stick with me, like a scar you can't quite forget.

The house had this small detached room with a bathroom in it, and it had bunk beds that we used to play around on. It felt separate from the rest of the house, like a little world of its own. John and I would sometimes sleep there together, just the two of us, trying to make sense of everything while the rest of the world felt like it was spinning out of control.

The main house was strange, too. There was this big room with glass walls, with layers almost like steps leading down to the main floor. It was the kind of room you'd expect to see a marching band practice in—except it was much smaller. The glass walls made everything feel exposed, like there was nowhere to hide, even though there was a lot we were all trying to hide from.

Danny and Vicky were Mormon, just like the family I'd end up with later. They didn't seem to care much for us, and I remember them being mean, cold. The kind of people who kept you at arm's length, making sure you knew your place wasn't with them.

Behind their house was a small canal with water running through it. In between the canal and the house was this hard dirt yard covered with thorns—sharp little bastards that would stick in your feet if you dared walk barefoot. I remember one time, the three of us were out playing in the canal. We were just kids, doing what kids do, splashing around and trying to make the best of wherever we were. Then this water snake swam past us, and we lost it.

We ran, all three of us, barefoot, across that hard dirt yard. By the time we made it back to the house, our feet were bloody, covered in thorns. But the pain in our feet was nothing compared to the kind of pain that was happening inside that house. I didn't realize it then, but Tasha was suffering more than John and I ever did. She was the girl in that house, and she bore the brunt of whatever cruelty Danny and Vicky had to give.

Tasha used to come into that small detached room with the bunk beds and the bathroom and sit on the toilet. I remember her sitting there, bleeding. I didn't understand what was happening at the time—she was too young to be going through puberty, too young for any of that. But the abuse was already taking its toll on her, in ways that I wouldn't fully comprehend until much later.

I don't remember how we were taken from that home. There's a blank space in my mind where the memory should be, and maybe it's better that way. All I know is that after that home, the three of us—John, Tasha, and I—were separated. We didn't see each other again for decades. I wouldn't see Tasha until I was 34 years old, and as for John, I never saw him again in person. The only contact we've had since then has been a few phone calls, as adults, trying to make sense of a past that still haunts us both.

After that home, I was taken to Terry and Teresa Richins in Morenci, Arizona. I was alone this time. John and Tasha were gone, sent somewhere else. All I had was a small white stuffed dog, a broken kids' game, and the clothes on my back. That's how I arrived at what would become my next prison—the Richins' home. I didn't know it yet, but this was the beginning of another kind of nightmare.

CHAPTER 4

Stripped of Safety

When I first arrived at the Richins' home in Morenci, Arizona, I was still **Joseph Monroe Robinson**. That was the name I had been given when I was born at Mount Shasta, California, to Johnny Clifton Robinson and Belinda Jean Camborn. It was the only piece of my identity that still felt like it was mine. But soon, even that would be taken away from me. I didn't know it yet, but the Richins would change everything about me, starting with my name.

When I met Terry Richins, there was a small part of me that felt safe. He wasn't overly affectionate or warm, but there was something in the way he carried himself that made me believe he wasn't going to hurt me. After everything I'd been through in the foster system, that feeling of safety was rare, and I clung to it. Terry seemed calm, almost gentle, in his own way. But whatever comfort I found in him didn't last long.

The moment I met Teresa, I knew things weren't going to be easy. She was cold, sharp, and distant from the start. No warmth in her voice, no softness in her eyes. Everything about her felt calculated, like she was already deciding how she could keep me in line. There was no room for mistakes in her world, and I was about to learn that the hard way.

On my first day in their house, I made a mistake. Not a huge one, just a small, innocent misstep—something you'd expect from a kid who had been passed from home to home, trying to figure out where he belonged. There was a small wooden stool in the house, and like any kid would, I sat on it. I didn't know the stool had been made specifically for Teresa. To me, it was just another piece of furniture. But when I scratched the top of it with my jean shorts, I learned quickly that in Teresa's house, even the smallest mistake would get you in trouble.

She didn't explode right away, but I could see it in her eyes—the irritation, the cold judgment. She was already marking me as a problem, and I hadn't even been there a full day.

Later that day, Teresa tried to play nice—or at least what passed for nice in her world. She set me up with a Super Nintendo and put on *Super Mario Brothers* for me to play. In those days, controllers weren't wireless, so I had to sit close to the TV, trying to lose myself in the game, hoping that maybe this house would be different. For a little while, I could almost pretend things were normal.

But I was still new, still adjusting. I didn't know all the rules yet, didn't know what was and wasn't okay. At one point in the game, I lost, and in my excitement, I yelled out, "Bastard!" I thought it was funny—didn't even know it was a bad word. I figured they'd laugh, maybe it would break the tension in the air. But instead, Teresa screamed at me.

Her voice was like a whip, cutting through the room, and before I knew what was happening, I was standing there, frozen, unsure of what I had done wrong. I didn't understand that in Teresa's house, there was no space for mistakes. I had only been **Joseph Monroe Robinson** for a few more days, and already, I was getting a taste of what life was going to be like as **T.J. Richins**.

That day was my introduction to the Richins' household, and it didn't take long for me to realize there would be no good days in that house. I hated Teresa from the very beginning.

Teresa played two roles. In public, around other people, she was kind, almost charming in her own way. She'd smile, laugh, and make it seem like everything was perfect. But behind closed doors, she was a different person entirely—bitter, sharp-tongued, and heavy-handed. The public never saw that side of her, but I did. Every day.

Terry was different, but even his kindness didn't provide any real safety. He didn't yell or hit, and for a while, I thought maybe he'd be the one to stand up for me. But as I soon found out, just because he wasn't the one doing the hurting didn't mean he was going to protect me. Teresa had a way of manipulating situations, twisting the truth to suit her narrative, and Terry, as gentle as he seemed, rarely stood up to her.

One time, I was in my small room—the space that was supposed to be mine but never felt like it. Outside my door was a closet where Teresa kept blankets and medicines. I overheard her talking to Terry that day, and I could tell from her tone that she was mad at me—again. She was always mad.

She opened the closet and pulled out a Tupperware container filled with empty anti-diarrheal pill wrappers. I watched as she calmly told Terry that *I* had taken the pills to lose weight. I was stunned, confused. I didn't even know people used those pills to lose weight. Terry stood there, looking just as confused as I was. We both knew the truth—those pills weren't mine. They had to be Teresa's. But in her twisted world, it didn't matter. She had decided that I was guilty, and that was the end of it.

That was just one example of how Teresa controlled the narrative, of how she made me the villain in her story. She was a high-standing Mormon wife, married to one of the supervisors at the mine where Terry worked. On the outside, she was the perfect wife and mother. But behind closed doors, I was the perfect target for her bitterness and rage.

Then came the day they made it official. I was no longer **Joseph Monroe Robinson**. The Richins had the judge change my name. Just like that, I became **Terrill Joseph Richins**, or **T.J.**, named after Terry, who wanted me to have the same initials as him. My middle name, **Joseph**, stayed, but everything else was gone.

They had taken my name, my last tie to who I had been before all of this. I was **T.J.** now, and even though they said I was part of their family, I never felt like it. I was **T.J. Richins**, but I wasn't. Not really. I was just the kid who couldn't do anything right, the one always in trouble, always on the receiving end of Teresa's anger.

CHAPTER 5

A Name Without a Family

When the judge officially changed my name to **Terrill Joseph Richins**, I didn't feel a thing. I stood there in the courtroom, the decision already made, and I didn't even smile. I remember Teresa getting upset about that—like not smiling meant I was ungrateful. But what was there to smile about? The name change didn't change anything in my heart. I wasn't attached to them, and they weren't attached to me. They weren't my parents. They were just another set of people who had power over me, and no matter what name I had, that power didn't come with love.

The day they changed my name, it wasn't just about the court ruling. After the adoption was finalized, they took me to the Mormon temple in Tempe, Arizona, for something called a "sealing." In their religion, being sealed meant I was now spiritually bound to them as if I had been born into the family. It was supposed to make me theirs in the eyes of God, to cement my place as one of their own.

I didn't want to be there. The whole process felt hollow, like a performance I was being forced into. Teresa was uptight the entire time, and I felt like I was walking on eggshells. I don't remember all the specifics, but what sticks with me is the scowl she had on her face. If it wasn't one thing, it was another with her. I didn't even want to be sealed to them, but I also didn't want them to be mad. There was no winning. No matter what I did, it was never enough. There was always something wrong with me in her eyes.

The trauma of living with Teresa was constant, but it wasn't always the big things that broke me down. It was the small, everyday moments—the comments, the scolding, the way she made me feel like I couldn't do anything right. I was too loud when I chewed my food. I smacked my lips too much when I ate. I looked angry when I wasn't. I needed to smile more. I needed to be quieter. It was always something. That kind of constant correction, that feeling that nothing about me was ever right, left deep scars that I still carry with me to this day.

And then, after the adoption and the sealing, things got worse. Teresa was more comfortable now, more free to do as she pleased. There were no more checkups from the state, no more social workers looking over her shoulder. I was hers now, and she knew it.

It wasn't long before they moved me to Cotton City, New Mexico—better known as Animas. It was miles from anywhere, isolated in the middle of nowhere. Terry's parents lived on a farm there, and we moved into the unused spare house on the same property. It was a lonely place, far removed from everything familiar. Terry was still a supervisor at the mine in Arizona, and eventually, we would move back to Morenci. But for those few years, Cotton City was my world, and it was a world full of abuse, isolation, and manipulation.

Cotton City was where Terry's extended family lived—his cousins, parents, aunts, and uncles. It was a tight-knit Mormon community, and Teresa had to keep up appearances. On the surface, everything looked fine. But behind the scenes, it was the same old story. Teresa found new ways to break me down. The isolation only made it worse. There were no neighbors close by, no one who might intervene. I was alone, trapped in that house with her, and the abuse continued.

Around the time I was nine, Teresa started driving me hours away to get therapy in Deming, New Mexico. I hated it. The therapy sessions forced me to dredge up things I was trying to forget, things my mind was desperately trying to bury. The therapist would make me play in a sandbox, as if that would somehow unlock the pain I carried. But I wasn't a normal kid. I had grown up too fast. I was far too old, emotionally, for sandbox therapy to do anything for me.

On one of those long drives to Deming, Teresa and I got into an argument. I don't remember what it was about—there were too many arguments to keep track of—but I do remember what happened next. She stopped the car in the middle of nowhere, on the side of the highway, and told me to get out. I was just a kid, standing there on the side of the road, and she drove off, leaving me behind. I was terrified. It was miles from anywhere, and for a moment, I thought she was really going to leave me there.

She did come back for me eventually, but the damage was done. What kind of person leaves a small boy on the side of the road like that? What kind of mother drives off and leaves a traumatized kid standing in the middle of nowhere?

Another time, it wasn't just her. Both Terry and Teresa were driving me to therapy, and again, they made me get out of the car. I wasn't going to get back in. I refused. I screamed, kicked, and threw my hands around, determined to make them see that I wasn't going to be treated like that anymore. Passing cars saw the scene unfold and thought I was being kidnapped. They called the cops. But I wasn't being saved that day. I was just a kid having another meltdown, trying to survive in a world that felt like it was constantly against me.

The trauma from those years is something I still carry. The bruises I had, both the visible ones and the ones you couldn't see, were always there. Even my friends at school noticed them sometimes. I tried to hide it, but you can only hide so much. And despite the abuse, despite the name change and the adoption, nothing ever changed for me emotionally. **T.J. Richins** wasn't a new start. It wasn't a new family. It was just another layer of pain.

CHAPTER 6

Humiliation as Control

By the time we moved to Cotton City, New Mexico, I had already spent years living with the Richins family. The isolation was something I was used to by then, but during my fourth-grade year, it became worse. Teresa decided to homeschool me that year, cutting me off from the world even more than before. She had control over everything I did—when I studied, when I had free time, when I could be a kid, if I could even be a kid at all. But with Teresa, even normal moments could become a form of punishment.

I still remember one birthday during that year. I must have been eight or nine years old. Teresa decided to throw me a party. She invited kids from church, set up games, prepared food, and even had a cake ready. At first, it looked like maybe, for once, I'd have a normal birthday. But this was Teresa we were talking about, and nothing with her was ever that simple.

I wasn't allowed to go to my own birthday party.

On the day of the party, she overloaded me with homework. I was homeschooled at the time, and she made sure that I had so much work, there was no way I'd finish it in time to enjoy the party. That was the rule: I couldn't join my own celebration until I finished my homework. I sat there, alone in the other room, while I could hear the sounds of the party—kids laughing, playing games, eating cake—everything happening without me. It was supposed to be my birthday, but it felt like a punishment.

I still remember my grandma Richins coming in to check on me. She lived just down the road and had come to the party like everyone else. She hugged me and told me happy birthday, and then, with a soft voice, she said, "It's wrong what she's doing to you." I knew she meant Teresa. Grandma could see through the facade Teresa put up for the rest of the family. She knew what was happening, but she also knew that Terry would never stand up to her. He always took Teresa's side, even when he knew she was wrong. And so, Grandma left, unable to change anything.

That year in Cotton City was a blur of isolation and control. Teresa's hold on me tightened, and it seemed like no matter what I did, I could never do anything right. But there were small moments when I felt connected to people. Terry's cousin, Melody Richins, lived nearby, and I was close to her and her kids. Melody treated me like part of the family. To her, I was just **T.J.**, her cousin—not the adopted kid, not the outsider. In her house, I could almost forget about everything Teresa put me through.

But even those small escapes were fragile.

There was one winter night, and it was snowing heavily in Cotton City. As usual, Teresa and I had gotten into a fight. It didn't matter what the fight was about—there were always fights with her. As punishment, she made me strip down to my underwear and sit outside, alone in the dark and snow. I sat there, freezing, too scared to do anything but follow her orders.

That night, Melody came over. She saw me sitting there, half-naked and shivering in the snow, but she didn't say anything. She didn't even look at me. It was like I wasn't there. I think she didn't want to start any drama with Teresa. Maybe it was easier for her to pretend she didn't see what was happening. But in that moment, it felt like even the small bit of safety I found in Melody's presence was gone.

Then there was Margot.

Margot was a beautiful girl from church. She had long red hair, and at the time, I had a crush on her. She was everything to me in that way kids have when they first start to notice someone. I looked forward to seeing her every week at church, and even though I didn't know how to talk to her or how to handle my feelings, she was one of the few bright spots in my life.

Of course, Teresa knew about it.

At the time, I was taking piano lessons, and Teresa would drive me to someone's house for the lessons. I'd practice at home, trying to master the songs, even though nothing I did was ever good enough for her. One day, Teresa decided I was acting like a baby. I don't even remember what I did to set her off, but she decided to humiliate me in the worst way possible.

She made me put on a diaper. Not just a diaper, but *only* a diaper. No clothes. I had to sit there, half-naked, humiliated and exposed, while she lectured me for whatever mistake I had made. And then, as if by "coincidence," Margot and her mom were invited over to the house. They arrived while I was still sitting there in just the diaper.

It was no coincidence. Teresa wanted to embarrass me in front of Margot, to make sure I felt as small and ashamed as possible. This wasn't about discipline—it was about control. And it worked. Margot never looked at me the same way again. I couldn't even look at her. The one girl I had a crush on, the one person who gave me a little bit of hope, saw me at my lowest, and I knew I would never be able to forget that.

That year was full of moments like that. Moments where Teresa took pleasure in tearing me down, in making sure I knew my place. Even though I was technically part of the family—**T.J. Richins**, the name that had been given to me—there was always something separating me from them. I could never be good enough, never do anything right.

Cotton City was a place of contradictions. On the one hand, I had moments with Melody and her family, where I felt like I was just **T.J.**, just their cousin. But on the other hand, I had Teresa, always watching, always waiting for me to mess up so she could remind me how much of an outsider I really was.

Eventually, we left Cotton City and moved back to Morenci, Arizona. That's when the isolation and control became even worse. But those years in Cotton City left a mark on me. They were the years where I learned that no matter how much you try to fit in, there are people who will always see you as less. And for Teresa, that was my role—to be less.

CHAPTER 7

Back in Morenci

Moving back to Morenci, Arizona, felt like a kind of relief. After spending a year isolated in Cotton City, being homeschooled by Teresa, it was a breath of fresh air to return to a place where I could be around other kids, some of whom I had known before we left. It felt good to have friends again. Sure, things had changed in the year I'd been gone, but I managed to reconnect with a few people and even make new friends.

There was Heather, who lived on the street below mine and was a year younger than me. We became fast friends. Then there was Daniel, who played the trumpet in marching band alongside me, living on the street above me. And, of course, Jessica—my best friend. We had this secret world we created together. We dabbled in magic spells and psychic stuff, the kind of thing that felt dangerous and thrilling in a small Mormon town like Morenci. We listened to music, drank Frappuccinos together—something that had to stay a secret since Mormons weren't supposed to drink coffee.

School became my escape, my sanctuary. It was the one place where I could be around my friends and not have to deal with Teresa's constant control. But even then, I wasn't free. I was different. I didn't fit the mold of a typical boy growing up in a small town. I was a bit girly, didn't do sports, and I often found myself on the receiving end of teasing and ridicule. But that didn't matter as much when I was with people like Jessica and Heather, who didn't care about any of that. They saw me for who I was, and for a little while, I could just be T.J.

Still, Teresa's control reached into every part of my life. While other kids got to go on field trips or enjoy after-school activities, I was rarely allowed to participate. There was always some reason why I couldn't go, why I had to stay within the immediate circle of the house. It was her way of keeping me under her thumb, of making sure I didn't have too much freedom. But even with those restrictions, I found ways to have fun. I remember sneaking out one night during middle school to hang out with some older kids. We went to a place on the outskirts of town called the corrals, where people kept their horses. I drank beer for the first time that night and got so drunk I could barely walk home.

When I got back, Teresa knew. She always knew. But instead of confronting me directly, she decided to make me suffer in silence. She told me to go inside and do the dishes right then and there, even though I was still throwing up from drinking. The next morning, she made a point of slamming the cabinet doors around the house, making as much noise as possible. She never brought up the drinking, but I knew that she knew. That was Teresa's way—punishment through manipulation, never outright addressing what was really happening.

Even at school, her control followed me. While the other kids got to eat lunch in the cafeteria, I had to walk all the way home to eat. She didn't give me lunch money, didn't even offer to pack me a lunch or give me a ride. I had to hurry back and forth, barely making it back to school on time. My friends, like Jessica and Heather, saw what was happening. They saw the bruises, sometimes firsthand. Heather's mom hated Teresa, and I'd sneak out to Heather's house to smoke a cigarette and escape the hell of my home life, if only for a little while.

There was never any escape from the big moments, though. Teresa always found a way to ruin the important days. Whether it was birthdays, proms, Christmas, or Halloween, she'd find some reason to ground me, making sure I missed out on any chance to feel like a normal kid. I wasn't allowed to go to prom. Every important event came with a punishment attached, and it felt like she was going out of her way to break me.

Even in marching band, where I found a small outlet of joy playing the trumpet, Teresa's humiliation found its way in. I was first trumpet—one of the best—and band practice took place out on the football field before school. One day, right in the middle of practice, Teresa drove up to the field. She had everyone stop practice, called me over, and made me stand in front of the entire band while she smelled my breath to see if I had been smoking pot. She called it "pot," even though I wasn't smoking anything. It was humiliating, standing there in front of all my classmates, as she made a scene. But that was Teresa. She never saw what she did as wrong—only as necessary to keep me in line.

The only real relief I found during those years came from my dad's younger sister, LaDonna. She was everything Teresa wasn't—wild, free, and unapologetically herself. LaDonna was the "bad sister" in the family, the one who drank, smoked, and went out to the country club on Friday nights to get drunk, hit on the guys, and play pool. She was the coolest person I knew. Sometimes, she'd take us kids with her to the country club because there was no one else to watch us. I'd sneak cigarettes from her freezer and steal cups of wine from the wine box.

LaDonna made me feel like I wasn't completely alone in the world. Her son, Duane, was my age, and we were close for a long time. We stayed tight until I got married to Hope and borrowed $300 from LaDonna's family that we never paid back. After that, everything changed. To this day, they hate me. Teresa even told me a few years ago that I wasn't welcome to live where they do because LaDonna's family doesn't want me around. It's been made clear that I need to stay away, and I've got no problem doing that.

But back then, LaDonna was my safe place. Her house was where I could go to feel normal, where my cousins and I could be kids without the constant weight of Teresa's anger hanging over us. Life was good when I was with them. I was part of something real, something that didn't come with conditions or punishment. I loved LaDonna, and for a while, it felt like maybe things could be okay.

But no matter where I went or who I spent time with, Teresa's hatred of me never left. She did everything she could to break me, and I could feel it in every interaction, every rule, every punishment. No matter how hard I tried to be good enough, to fit in, it was never enough for her. She hated me, and she didn't bother to hide it.

CHAPTER 8

A Dark Turn in High School

High school started off as a mix of hope and darkness for me. As a freshman, I was still trying to find my place, but there was something that set me apart from everyone else. I had started attending modeling school at Barbizon in Tucson, Arizona. For once, I felt like I had something special, something that made me stand out. Going to modeling school was a way to escape the weight of my home life, a way to feel like I could be someone different, someone admired.

Every so often, Teresa would come pick me up from school in her brand-new red Ford Excursion, a huge, flashy car that seemed to announce her importance. Sometimes she'd bring along her friend Janie, her sister Janice, or even her mother, Grandma Turner. They'd drive me to Tucson for modeling school, and for a few hours, I'd be away from everything—away from the constant criticism and control. While I was at the school, learning how to walk the runway, pose for photos, and present myself to the world, Teresa and her crew would go shopping, spending the day treating themselves while I worked on creating an image that felt like mine.

I remember the final photo shoot at Barbizon like it was yesterday. Dozens of amazing photos were taken of me, all moments frozen in time that could have been mine to keep. But when it came time to buy the photos, they only allowed me to choose one. Just one picture out of all the memories that could have been preserved. Teresa decided that was all I could have.

Even though I felt like I had something good in modeling, something that made me feel special, it wasn't enough to drown out the darker parts of my life that were starting to surface. As high school went on, I started to change, to shift into someone I barely recognized. I was drawn to the darker side of things, finding comfort in rebellion and new friendships that took me far away from the good kid I had once been.

I became gothic, dressing in black, wearing heavy eyeliner, and leaning into the identity of someone who didn't fit in with the rest of the world. I started hanging around with people who didn't judge me for being different, who accepted me for who I was becoming. That's when I met Melissa and Rachel. They became my two best friends, and for a while, I felt like I had found my people. They were funny, rebellious, and unapologetically themselves. But they also introduced me to something that would change my life forever—meth.

It started off small, just experimenting, just trying something new. But soon, I was hooked. I didn't realize how deep I was sinking into it until it was too late. Melissa and Rachel made me feel like I belonged, but the cost was steep. Meth became an addiction, a way to numb the pain of everything I had been carrying for so long—the abuse, the isolation, the constant feeling of never being good enough.

I started stealing from Terry and Teresa. Little things at first—money, valuables—anything I could trade to get more meth. I ditched school constantly, slipping further and further away from the person I had been. It wasn't long before I got caught and was sent to juvenile detention. I was sixteen years old.

In juvie, I hit rock bottom, but I also discovered something unexpected—I was smart. I got my GED while I was there, and not just a passing score. I earned the highest score possible. It was like a glimpse of who I could have been, the potential that still existed under all the layers of pain and bad choices. But by then, I had already made up my mind—I was done with school, done with trying to fit into a world that didn't seem to want me.

When I turned eighteen, I wasted no time. The morning of my eighteenth birthday, I packed up my things and moved out of the house. I got a job at the local grocery store and began carving out a life of my own, free from Teresa's control for the first time in my life. But even with the freedom, I was still battling the demons that had taken root inside me during those dark high school years.

That's when **Hope** came back into my life.

We had met in middle school, and even back then, we had been close. She had moved to Louisiana when we were sixteen, and for a while, we lost touch. But when she moved back to Arizona, it was like no time had passed at all. We were inseparable. Hope was everything I needed at that time in my life—someone who didn't see the broken parts of me, someone who loved me despite everything.

We got married when I was eighteen, and Hope was nineteen. Our relationship felt like the one good thing I had. We built a life together, and not long after, Caleb was conceived. I still think back to the night he was conceived—the night that would change everything. I was twenty years old, and Hope was nineteen. We were married, building a life, and for a while, it felt like maybe I had finally escaped the darkness that had followed me for so long.

Hope and her mother, Noreen, were inseparable, just like Hope and I were. In those early years of marriage, life seemed full of possibilities. But the shadows of the past were never far away. The addiction, the trauma, the pain—they were all still there, just waiting for their chance to come back into my life.

CHAPTER 9

Young, Wild, and Scared

The morning I turned eighteen, I was ready. I had my stuff packed for days, waiting for the moment I could finally leave Teresa and Terry's house behind me. I didn't care about the note she left me, that cold farewell wrapped in a basket with soap and a washcloth. It was her way of saying, "Good luck"—but I didn't need it. I was out. I was free, or at least, I thought I was.

Not long after I moved out, I found out that **Hope** had moved back to Arizona. She was living in a nearby town called Safford with her mom, **Noreen**. We had lost touch when she moved to Louisiana during high school, but as soon as I knew she was back, I couldn't stay away. I'd drive the hour-long trip to Safford just to see her, then drive back the same night. We were inseparable. Every time we said goodbye, we'd cry—like it physically hurt us to be apart. That's how close we were.

It wasn't long before we were married. Hope was nineteen, and I was twenty. It felt like we had the whole world in front of us, that we could do anything. We were young, wild, and reckless. We did everything together—meth, drinking, staying up all night. Life felt like it would last forever, like nothing could stop us.

That same day we got married, we found out that Hope was pregnant. I remember how strange it was, how surreal. I was just twenty years old, and suddenly, I was going to be a father. I wasn't sure how to feel. A part of me was terrified, but another part of me felt something I hadn't felt in a long time—hope. It was like I finally had something that was mine, something I could protect and love, something no one could take from me.

But life didn't give us much time to settle into the idea of being parents. Hope's pregnancy went smoothly, but right after she gave birth to our son **Caleb**, she found out she had **Myasthenia Gravis**. Everything changed. We had barely had time to enjoy being newlyweds, to have that "just us" phase, before we were thrown into a whirlwind of medical appointments, surgeries, and stress. It was a lot for anyone, let alone two kids who were still trying to figure out how to be adults.

We had to move to Tucson for a while, staying with Hope's older sister Cindy while Hope underwent serious surgeries. I remember feeling overwhelmed, like everything was happening too fast. We had this tiny, helpless newborn to care for, and on top of that, Hope was sick. Caleb had to go through it all with us, bouncing from hospital rooms to Cindy's house, trying to make sense of a world that felt out of control.

That's when Terry and Teresa started stepping in. At first, it seemed like they were just trying to help. They'd offer to take Caleb for a few days while we dealt with Hope's health issues. At the time, I was grateful. I was young, scared, and overwhelmed with everything that was happening. It made sense to let them help. But looking back, I think that's when something sparked in them. Something that would, a year or so later, turn into them taking Caleb from me permanently.

During those early years, being a father was strange and beautiful. I was scared—I didn't know what the hell I was doing. But I was also so gentle with Caleb. I used to fall asleep with him lying next to me in bed, something I know now is dangerous, but back then, it felt normal. It felt like love. We had a white bassinet for him in our small apartment in Safford, and I remember the way he looked sleeping in it, like he was the only thing in the world that mattered.

In those first months, I changed. I had finally found something of my own—something no one could take away from me. Caleb was mine, and I was determined to be the father I had never had. I wanted to protect him, love him, and make sure he never felt the kind of pain I had felt growing up. I wasn't perfect—far from it—but in those moments with Caleb, I felt like I had found a purpose, something real to hold onto in a world that often felt so uncertain.

But life kept moving, and the struggles didn't go away. The stress of Hope's illness, the chaos of trying to be young parents while still figuring out who we were, and the pressures of addiction all loomed over us. We were kids raising a kid, and while we loved each other, it wasn't enough to keep the darkness from creeping back in. Still, for those brief moments, being a father changed me. It gave me something to fight for, something to love. And for a while, it was enough.

CHAPTER 10

The Beginning of the End

There was one moment, one day, that still sticks with me—a day when the weight of everything came crashing down all at once. Hope was in the hospital, facing one of the scariest surgeries of her life. They called it a sternectomy or sternotomy—I can't even remember exactly, just that it meant they had to open her chest. There was this looming fear that she might not make it out alive. It was the kind of fear that hits you deep in your core and makes everything else seem small. I was only twenty, still a kid myself, raising a newborn while my wife faced death.

I had Caleb with me in Tucson, just a tiny baby, and I felt like I was drowning. I didn't know what to do. I didn't feel ready to handle all of this alone. It felt like the trauma I had been carrying since childhood had bubbled up, and I was on the verge of losing control. So I did the only thing I could think of—I called Teresa.

Tucson was a four-hour drive from Morenci, but she agreed to come and get Caleb. She called her sister Janice to see if she would come with her, and Janice had to take off work to make the trip. They got halfway to Tucson when I called them back. The panic attack was over, the moment of fear had passed, and I told them not to worry about it—I was fine, I could handle it. I thought that was the end of it.

But it wasn't. That one moment set off a chain of resentment that I didn't see coming.

Janice was furious. She had taken off work, lost money, and now I was telling her it was for nothing. Teresa wasn't happy either, and the worst part was that Teresa hated me simply because Janice did. That's how Teresa worked—she was a people pleaser, always looking for approval from those around her. And in that moment, Janice's anger became Teresa's anger. I didn't realize it at the time, but that moment built a foundation of resentment that would eventually grow into something far worse.

After that, whenever Terry and Teresa took Caleb for "help," they would start keeping him for longer stretches. The excuses came quickly: Tucson was too far away, it cost too much to drive back and forth, so if they were going to take him, it had to be for at least a week—sometimes two. It felt like they were taking more and more control over Caleb's life, but at the time, I didn't see it for what it was. I was still too young, too overwhelmed, and too focused on just surviving each day.

Caleb turned one, then one and a half, and by that point, Hope's health had improved enough for us to leave Tucson. We moved in with an old friend of mine named Patricia. She let us stay in her garage while we got back on our feet, but it was winter, and the cold was brutal. Snow piled up outside, and the garage was freezing—much too cold for a baby. It wasn't the life we wanted for Caleb, but we were trying. We were doing the best we could with what we had.

That's when Terry and Teresa swooped in like the saviors they always pretended to be. They offered to take Caleb again, just temporarily, until Hope and I could get things settled. At the time, I was still blinded by trust. I didn't see their real intentions, and I thought they were just helping. I believed them when they said it was temporary.

Then came the mistake that changed everything.

One day, while Patricia was out, I got curious. I snuck into one of the rooms in her house and took a VHS tape. I don't even know why I did it. I was bored, I guess, and looking for something to do. Hope didn't know what I had done. She knew I had gone into the room, but she had no idea I had taken anything. When Patricia came home and noticed the tape was missing, she asked me if I took it, and I lied. Of course, I lied. But she wasn't stupid. She searched the garage where we were staying, found the tape, and kicked us out immediately.

We had nowhere to go. Terry and Teresa came to the rescue again, or at least that's how it seemed. They had Janice babysit Caleb while they helped Hope and me move out of Patricia's garage. It felt like they were saving us once again, stepping in to make sure Caleb was taken care of while we figured things out. That's when they presented us with paperwork.

They told us it was just for insurance, just in case something happened to Caleb while he was with them. I didn't think twice about it. I was so used to trusting them, so used to believing that they had Caleb's best interests at heart. We signed the papers without reading them—why would we? They were family. We thought they were helping.

It wasn't until later, when we tried to get Caleb back, that we found out the truth. Those papers weren't just for insurance. They were legal guardianship papers. We had unknowingly signed our child away.

The realization hit like a freight train. We had been tricked, manipulated into giving up our son without even knowing it. By the time we understood what had happened, it was too late. Terry and Teresa had the legal right to keep Caleb, and no matter how hard we fought, we couldn't undo what had been done.

In that moment, I felt something break inside me. Caleb was the one thing I had, the one thing I had sworn I would never let anyone take from me. And yet, there he was—gone. Stolen. And there was nothing I could do about it.

CHAPTER 11

An Impossible Fight

When I first realized that Caleb had been taken from me—legally, with no way to just take him back—it didn't hit me all at once. Terry and Teresa didn't make it obvious right away. They made it seem like it was still temporary, like it was all part of a plan to help Hope and me get back on our feet. In their way, they offered us a path forward, a way to earn Caleb back. But every time we got close, they'd move the goalpost, adding more impossible tasks to the list.

First, it was simple enough: get a stable job. Then, it was keep that job for a year straight. After that, it was get your own car. Then your own house. Stop smoking. Don't drink. The list kept growing, and each new requirement felt more impossible than the last. It wasn't just about getting Caleb back anymore—it was about breaking us down, slowly making sure we knew we would never be good enough in their eyes.

But we didn't stop trying. We didn't give up right away. Hope and I did everything we could to prove to them that we could be the parents Caleb deserved. We worked, we saved, we tried to get back on our feet, even as the odds stacked higher and higher against us. The pressure was relentless, and no matter what we did, it was never enough. Still, I kept trusting them. I believed—*wanted* to believe—that if we just did what they said, they'd give Caleb back. That if we were good enough, they'd let us be a family again.

But somewhere deep down, I knew the truth. Teresa wasn't going to give him back. She had finally gotten the baby she couldn't have on her own, and now that she had him, she wasn't going to let him go. Caleb was her chance to mold the perfect Mormon child, to give Terry the son they never had. In her mind, she was the mother now, and nothing I did would change that.

By the time Hope and I moved to Globe, Arizona, we were barely holding on. The strain of trying to meet Terry and Teresa's impossible demands, combined with the weight of losing Caleb, was too much. Our relationship started to fracture under the pressure. We were young, broken, and buried deep in addiction. Meth and alcohol became our way of numbing the pain, of getting through each day without collapsing under the weight of everything we'd lost.

Living in Globe was a blur. We were relying on the help of friends just to survive, scraping by however we could. Hope and I used the label of Mormon to get help from the church, even though neither of us was truly a member. We needed the help, and in those desperate times, I wasn't above claiming the Richins name when it was convenient. But that name—**Richins**—was no longer mine. I was **Derrick Bullock** now, and cutting their name from my life made Terry and Teresa furious. It was one more wedge driven between us, one more way they could justify keeping Caleb.

Even after everything, even after they had stolen him, I kept trusting them. I kept holding on to the hope that if I could just meet their expectations, they'd give him back. But somewhere deep inside, I knew the truth. Teresa was never going to let that happen. She had Caleb, and that was all she had ever wanted. A baby she could raise as her own, a child to mold into the perfect little Mormon, a son she could give to Terry. I wasn't a part of that picture anymore.

They had stolen my son, and no matter how much I tried to fight it, no matter how hard Hope and I worked to get him back, it was never going to happen. Teresa had won. She had taken the one thing I had sworn I would never lose, and there was nothing I could do to stop it.

CHAPTER 12

The End of Us

When Hope and I moved to Globe, Arizona, it was supposed to be a fresh start. After everything that had happened with Caleb, after the pressure and strain of trying to meet Terry and Teresa's impossible demands, we thought maybe we could rebuild, maybe we could find a way to make it work. But it didn't take long to realize that our marriage was already falling apart.

We moved in with my best friend at the time, **Donna**. She had been there for me before, and once again, she opened her home to Hope and me. But living with Donna didn't bring us the stability we were searching for. Instead, it became a place where we sank deeper into our addictions. Every night, Donna would buy me beer with the little money she had, and every night, I would pass out drunk. It was a cycle that numbed the pain, but it didn't fix anything. If anything, it made everything worse.

I didn't know how to cope with the loss of Caleb. I didn't know how to deal with the anger and betrayal I felt. I was furious at Terry and Teresa for stealing my son, but I was also furious at myself for not seeing it sooner. The alcohol was my escape, but it was also fueling the worst parts of me. I was angry all the time—at Hope, at the world, at myself. I yelled, I cussed, I screamed. I broke things. I intimidated her, pushed her away, and in the process, destroyed whatever small chance we had left of holding onto our marriage.

At some point during that time, I reached out to a Mormon couple in Globe. They were older, and they owned a doublewide trailer at the top of the hill overlooking the whole park. I used the **Richins name** to get their attention, still relying on the Mormon label to get by, even though I had cut myself off from them. They let us rent the trailer for cheap, and Hope and I moved in. It was empty—no furniture, nothing to make it feel like a home—but it was ours. It was a place where, for a moment, we thought maybe we could start over.

But it wasn't enough. The glue that had once held us together—the love we had shared, the bond that had made us inseparable—was gone. By that point, we had both cheated on each other, with both men and women. The trust was shattered, and we were different people than we had been when we first got married. There was nothing left to hold us together except the weight of the past, and that wasn't enough.

I was abusive. I won't sugarcoat it. I was angry, and I took that anger out on Hope. I yelled at her, made her feel small, used my rage to intimidate her. I was broken, and I didn't know how to fix it. I couldn't handle the pain I was feeling, so I buried it with alcohol, buried it with anger. But it only pushed Hope further away.

It wasn't long before she decided she couldn't take it anymore. She wanted a divorce, and I couldn't blame her. We weren't a family anymore. We were just two people stuck in a cycle of pain, addiction, and betrayal. Her mom, **Noreen**, drove up from Safford to come get her. I still remember that moment clearly—I was in the back room of the house, handing Hope her belongings through the open window. She didn't want to come inside, and her mom was being overprotective, making sure everything went her way. She milked it, making a scene out of the whole thing.

I cried, of course. I had loved Hope. We had built a life together, but that life was crumbling, and there was nothing left to hold onto. I buried the pain the only way I knew how—with alcohol. It was easier to drown in it than to face the reality of everything I had lost. Hope, Caleb, the family we had tried to build—it was all gone, and I was left alone in the empty doublewide, trying to figure out what the hell I was supposed to do next.

That's when Donna introduced me to **Brian Ortiz**.

Brian would go on to become my best friend for the next few years. He was someone who understood me in ways that others didn't. We bonded quickly, and before long, we were inseparable. We ended up living together, and for a while, it felt like maybe I had found a new family—someone who wouldn't leave, someone who wouldn't betray me. Brian became the person I leaned on as I tried to rebuild my life, but even with his friendship, the pain of losing Caleb and Hope never fully went away.

The breakdown of my marriage with Hope marked the end of one chapter in my life. But it was also the beginning of a new chapter—one filled with more pain, more struggles, and more battles I wasn't prepared for.

CHAPTER 13

Brother in Chaos

After Hope left, I was alone for a few months. It was a strange and lonely time, filled with the kind of emptiness that comes when you lose both a marriage and a child. I didn't know where to turn, and I drowned myself in alcohol to make the pain disappear, even if just for a while. But then I met **Brian Ortiz**, and everything changed.

Brian had been friends with **Donna** for years. He lived with his dad at the time in a run-down house just down the road from the trailer park. The first time I met him, I thought he was beautiful. He was an outcast, full of anxiety, and psychic—just like me. We even shared the same birthday, which made it feel like we were twins, except he was Hispanic and I was white. He had these naturally thick eyelashes that made him look like he was always wearing eyeliner. I was immediately drawn to him.

Brian was with a girl named **Michelle** when I first met him. She was a few years younger than him, a fiery Hispanic girl, and they had a newborn daughter together. But their relationship was toxic. They fought constantly, and it wasn't just yelling. Michelle would hit him, they'd scream at each other, and the cops would get called. She'd leave, then come back, and the cycle would repeat. It was chaos, but I was already living in chaos, so it didn't seem all that unusual at the time.

At first, both Brian and Michelle moved in with me. I had the master bedroom, and they stayed on the other side of the house with their baby. It was a strange setup, but it worked for about six months to a year. During that time, Brian and I became inseparable. He wasn't just a friend—he was like a brother to me. We smoked weed together, we drank heavily, and he became the reason I got through those dark years after losing Hope and Caleb.

Eventually, the three of us decided to leave Globe behind and move to **Mesa, Arizona**. We found a nice apartment on the second floor of **Lakeview Apartments**, a beautiful complex with multiple pools, a gym, and lakes that surrounded the property. It was right on the outskirts of Mesa, so we had access to everything the city had to offer. I thought maybe it was a fresh start, a chance to finally build something stable.

But things weren't as simple as moving to a new place. Even in Mesa, I was still dealing with the consequences of my past. Before Hope and I had moved to Globe, I had committed identity theft. I found someone's information online and used it to buy furniture at **Ashley Furniture** in **Safford, Arizona**. I got caught, of course, and it landed me a felony charge. The legal fallout from that crime followed me to Mesa, and part of my sentence was that I had to spend four months in jail—only on weekends.

Every Friday, I'd make the drive from Mesa back to Safford and spend the weekend in jail. Then I'd drive back to Mesa during the week, trying to live some kind of normal life in between. It was exhausting, but I had no choice. I had to serve my time.

During that time, I was also fighting for **social security benefits**. My PTSD, manic depression, bipolar disorder, and anxiety disorder had left me unable to work consistently, and after months of waiting, my application was finally approved. I was awarded $14,000, a back payment for the time I had been struggling with my mental health since I was 18. At the time, it felt like a lot of money. I kept it in a black laptop bag and carried it with me wherever I went, even when I was driving to jail on the weekends. The bag sat in the trunk of my car while I served my time, and when I was finally done with jail, it felt like maybe I had a fresh start ahead of me.

That's when Brian, Michelle, and I decided to take a trip to **Hollywood, California**. I had bought a silver **Chevy Lumina** with some of my social security money, and we used it to drive out to California for the weekend. For the first time in a long time, it felt like we were free, like we had escaped the weight of our lives back in Arizona.

Hollywood was everything I thought it would be—chaotic, colorful, and full of life. We walked down the Hollywood Walk of Fame, seeing the stars on the sidewalk with famous names that I had only ever seen on TV. I even got to see inside a famous theater, something I had always dreamed of. We stayed at one of the well-known hotels on Hollywood Boulevard, and for that weekend, it felt like we were living in a different world.

Of course, we partied. We drank heavily, smoked weed, and I even hooked up with a random guy I met on the strip. I got my lip pierced that weekend, a symbol of the wild, rebellious freedom I was feeling. It was a reckless weekend, but at the time, it felt like the start of something better, something new.

But even with the fun and freedom of Hollywood, there was still something missing. The chaos followed me wherever I went, and as much as I tried to escape it, I couldn't shake the feeling that everything I was doing was just a distraction. The pain of losing Caleb, the collapse of my marriage with Hope, and the weight of all the bad decisions I had made still hung over me, no matter how far I ran.

Brian's friendship was the only thing that kept me grounded during those years. He was there when I needed someone, a brother in the middle of all the chaos. But even with him by my side, the darkness was still there. The drinking, the partying, the reckless decisions—it was all a way to numb the pain I hadn't yet figured out how to deal with.

CHAPTER 14

Running and Escaping

Before we left California to head back to Arizona, we had one last wild night that perfectly captured the chaos of my life during that time. We decided to eat at this expensive sushi restaurant, the kind of place that had a crazy long line just to get a table. It was one of those places where you eat like kings—plates stacked high with every kind of sushi you can imagine, saki flowing like water, and raw seafood that made you feel like you were tasting something from another world.

The meal was incredible, but it came with a price. It was expensive, and I was prepared to pay for it. But then, out of nowhere, Brian and Michelle got up and ran. I had no idea what was going on. It was like they had planned it without me. I was caught off guard, but the adrenaline kicked in, and I followed them, running down the street toward my car. It was parked at the end of a dead-end road, facing the beach.

We jumped into my silver **Chevy Lumina** under the cover of night. My heart was pounding as we pulled away, but to get back on the main road, we had to drive right by the restaurant. As we passed, I could see the staff looking for us, but we weren't caught. We got away with it, and even though it was reckless, it made for a wild memory, one that I'll never forget.

When we got back to the apartment in Mesa, life was already changing. I had met someone new—a man named **Justin Jones**, who lived in **North Scottsdale**, not too far from where I lived. I had met him on a gay hookup app, and we started seeing each other. Justin was different.

He was an online entrepreneur, running his own adult cam company. He hired models to perform for clients online and paid them based on the traffic they pulled in. It sounded lucrative, and at first, I was impressed.

Justin drove a red **Lexus**, which I assumed he had bought with money from his business. He seemed like someone who had everything together—successful, driven, and connected. He had friends all over the Valley because he installed touchscreens at gay bars across the area. He was well-known, and sometimes he'd take me with him when he went out to these places, introducing me to people.

I started staying over at Justin's house more and more. We'd hook up, watch movies, and hang out, and soon enough, I realized I wanted a change. I was tired of the chaos with Brian and Michelle. I wanted something new, something that felt like it had more stability—even if it was just an illusion. So I made the decision to leave Brian and Michelle behind. I moved in with Justin, leaving the apartment under Michelle's name. I didn't really know what happened to them after that, but at the time, it didn't seem to matter. I had moved on to a new chapter.

Living with Justin wasn't exactly what I thought it would be. It didn't take long for me to realize that his business wasn't making money like I had thought. Justin had **AIDS**, and he was living off a disability check he had received after being diagnosed. That's how he had bought his **Mac desktop**, how he was renting the house, and how he had bought his Lexus. The cam business wasn't lucrative—it was a front. He kept up appearances, but the reality was far less glamorous.

Despite this, Justin had something I admired—**drive**. He was motivated, always working on something, always meeting new people and networking. Even though he was an alcoholic, he still managed to keep things moving forward, and in some ways, I was drawn to that energy. He had friends everywhere, and while I knew after a few months that he was hooking up with some of the guys we met at the bars, I didn't really care. I knew he wasn't my soulmate. He was just a new place to stay, a way to escape the life I had left behind.

Justin had a roommate named **Nick Prada**, who was about as different from Justin as you could get. Nick was a ladies' man, always bringing different women home, partying late into the night. He was a male dancer, and his life revolved around clubs, bars, and the kind of wild nightlife that felt exciting but exhausting at the same time. There were nights when Nick would bring home women, they'd bang loudly in the next room, and I'd lie there in bed listening to the chaos. The house was always full of energy, always buzzing with parties, drugs, and noise.

At first, it was fun. The chaos of Nick's life felt like an extension of my own. It was loud, it was messy, but it was distracting. For a while, it kept me from thinking too much about everything I had lost. But after a few months of living in that constant party atmosphere, I started to see through it. The fun started to wear off, and the reality of what my life had become started to sink in.

I was living in a house with a man who wasn't my soulmate, surrounded by people who were just as lost as I was. The parties, the drinking, the hookups—it was all a distraction from the emptiness I was feeling inside. I didn't know what I was looking for, but I knew it wasn't this.

CHAPTER 15

Caught in the Web

Things were already starting to fall apart between me and **Justin**. By this point, I had begun pulling away from him. We were living in the same house, but the dynamic had shifted. It was clear that Justin saw me as *his*. Not in a romantic way—he didn't want to sleep with me—but he didn't want anyone else to have me, either. It was a possessive control that would become a theme in my life over the next few relationships.

I ended up moving into the spare room on the other side of Justin. The house was laid out with three bedrooms—**Nick** had the room on the right, Justin's was in the middle, and I had the room on the left. For a while, we pretended things were fine, but it was obvious that things were becoming strained. Justin was still running his adult cam business from the house, and I had been hired as one of his cam models. **Nick** was camming too, along with a few other models who worked for Justin. The house had become a hub of activity, with people coming and going, setting up cam sessions, and spending hours performing for clients online.

Despite all of this, Justin still had another job on the side—helping his dad with his failing business. He was trying to save the business, but it was a losing battle. I helped out by organizing paperwork, trying to keep things together, but I could feel that my role in his life was shifting. I wasn't just a roommate. I was his "little bitch," doing whatever he needed, helping him with the cam business and his dad's work, all while living under his roof.

That's when **Austin** came into the picture.

Justin had known Austin from his network and hired him as one of his cam models. Austin was in his late twenties, bald, covered in tattoos, and had an incredible body—muscular and defined, with tattoos that stretched across his chest, back, legs, and even his ass. He had piercing blue eyes that contrasted sharply with his rough appearance. He wasn't attractive in the traditional sense—his face was far from pretty—but his body made up for it.

One day, Justin asked me to help him with Austin's initiation photoshoot. Austin needed pictures for his online cam profile, and Justin wanted them to be perfect. While his dad was away, Justin brought me and Austin to the office where the photoshoot was set up. Austin got completely naked, and Justin handed me a bottle of oil. My job was to rub the oil all over Austin's body, making sure he glistened in the sunlight. I could feel the tension in the room as I worked, trying to keep it professional but failing miserably. I was turned on, and it was clear that Justin was too, though we both pretended otherwise.

Once Austin was oiled up, I held up a reflective screen while Justin took photos of him posing against a chain-link fence. It was surreal—this incredibly sexualized atmosphere, but with this strange unspoken tension between the three of us. It felt like a line was being crossed, but none of us acknowledged it.

A few months later, Austin started camming from our house. Justin had turned the living room into Austin's cam room, setting up room dividers to give him some privacy. But **privacy** wasn't something Austin cared much about. He was loud, unapologetically so. When he was camming, he'd moan loudly, making enough noise that the neighbors could probably hear. He didn't cam with other people—he was a solo performer—but it didn't matter. His presence in the house was disruptive, and the noise became a constant reminder of the strange life we were all living.

It didn't take long for things to escalate between me and Austin. The tension that had started during that initial photoshoot grew over time, and eventually, we found ourselves getting into trouble together.

CHAPTER 16

Breaking Point

Things between me and **Justin** had already started to fall apart, but that one night is where it all came to a head. Justin had gone out to the club with one of his closest friends, **Sam**—one of his best cammers. Sam was over often, and their friendship had always seemed strong. While Justin and Sam were out, I was camming from my room, and **Austin** was in the living room, camming like usual—loud, obnoxious, and impossible to ignore.

His moans echoed through the house, and after a while, I couldn't take it anymore. I called him into my room. The tension between us had been building for months, ever since that first photoshoot where I oiled him up for his cam profile. That night, I topped him, and afterward, we found ourselves heading into Justin's bedroom with a laptop in hand. We were drunk, reckless, and no longer thinking clearly. We cammed together on Justin's bed—something I never imagined I would do, but in that moment, nothing seemed real.

We were still drunk and stumbling when we ended up in the kitchen, making out, when Justin and Sam came home. Sam had to carry Justin to bed—he was blacked out drunk, thank god. He didn't see anything, but Sam did. She saw us, and for a moment, our eyes locked. But she never said a word about it. That's how everything was in Justin's world—unspoken, hidden, but always there, just below the surface.

Later that same night, Austin and I walked down the road to a huge park with a pond, a quiet place filled with ducks and open space. We sat together on a bench, the cool night air wrapping around us, and it felt like, for a moment, we were the only two people in the world. That's when things went further—I wasn't thinking, just reacting, and we ended up together on that park bench. By the time we finished, the adrenaline was wearing off, and we decided to head back home.

When we got there, the door was locked. In a rare moment of clarity, I had left my bedroom window open before we left. Thank god for that. We had to climb in through the window to get back into the house. That night was the beginning of the end.

The next morning, Justin drove Austin home. He didn't say anything to him, but when he got back, he told me he knew what had happened. I wasn't surprised. I looked him in the eye and told him the truth—**we hadn't been together for months**, not in any real sense. Our relationship had been over for a long time, so what did it matter?

After that, we had a moment of clarity between us. We weren't a couple, and we made it clear that whatever was left between us was purely transactional—me living in his house, helping out with the cam business. That was all that remained. Still, I stayed living there. Even though everything was crumbling, I didn't have anywhere else to go, and as chaotic as it was, it felt like the only life I had.

But it wasn't long before the weight of everything became too much. The drinking, the chaos, the failed relationships—it all crashed down on me at once. I was spiraling, lost in a world that was slipping further out of control. In a drunken stupor, I made the decision to end it all. I grabbed the bottles of medication I had—**antidepressants, sleep aids, and anti-anxiety pills**—and took them all at once.

At first, I didn't feel anything. But as time passed, the regret hit me. I realized I didn't want to die. I wanted to take it back, but it was too late. I started throwing up, blue foam spilling from my mouth and staining the white carpet beneath me. It's strange, the things you remember. The carpet was ruined, that bright blue stain never leaving it. But I didn't care about the carpet. I was terrified. I had gone too far, and I couldn't undo it.

Justin found me lying on the bed. He tried to wake me up, slapped me a few times, even did a sternum rub, but I didn't respond. I was already too far gone. I woke up three or four days later in the **ICU**. I had no memory of getting there. My body was weak, my mind cloudy, and I had to learn to walk again, to speak properly. It felt like I had been erased, only to be written back into existence.

While I was in the ICU, Justin called my adopted family, thinking I wouldn't make it. He told them what had happened, and **Teresa** came to see me. She wasn't there out of love or concern, but out of curiosity—probably waiting for me to die. But in that moment, on what felt like my deathbed, I told her something I had been holding inside for a long time. Something I had never had the courage to say before.

CHAPTER 17

The ICU and the Second Fall

Waking up in the **ICU** after my first suicide attempt was like emerging from a fog. Everything was hazy—my mind felt like it had been erased and rewritten in a blur. The room was dimly lit, high up on some floor in a hospital in **Tempe, Arizona**. I had wires and IVs hooked up to me everywhere, and a catheter, too. I could barely talk, having just been taken off the intubator. I felt like a ghost tethered to a hospital bed.

Even though everything was foggy, I remember who was there. Standing to the right of the bed, I saw faces I hadn't expected—people who I hadn't thought would come to see me. **My dad's older sister Carolyn** was there, one of the few family members I had fond memories of. She was a fun aunt, the one who would sometimes take me for entire summers, and I always looked forward to those summers. Seeing her there, in the middle of all this darkness, was a brief spark of comfort.

Terry was there too, but my focus went straight to **Teresa**, standing closest to me, holding my hand as if she was some loving, doting mother. It pissed me off. She was only there for show, for the attention. If I had died, she would've milked it for everything it was worth, telling people what a "good" son I was and how much I was loved. She would have twisted it to her advantage, like she always did.

I remember **Justin** being there, too, and I think the Mormon bishop was there at some point, but everything was still so unclear. What I do remember is that I couldn't take Teresa's fake affection anymore. I pulled my right hand out of hers, my body feeling like it was strapped to the bed like a mummy. Even though I could barely speak, I managed to tell her the truth I had been holding in for so long: **she never loved me**, and everything about her was fake. I didn't have the strength to scream, but the words hit hard. I kicked her out of the room, telling her to never visit or call again.

She didn't fight me on it. The moment she realized I wasn't going to die, she had no problem complying with my request. That was Teresa—there when it served her, gone when it didn't.

After my release from the hospital, **Justin** took me back in. For a brief moment, things felt like they were getting better. But the hospital had put me right back on the same medications I had used to try and end my life, with no supervision. So, nothing really changed. The environment hadn't shifted—**Justin** was still there, acting like my caretaker, trying to manage everything. It became overwhelming all over again.

The darkness that had driven me to the first suicide attempt still hung over me, and it didn't take long for me to spiral again. A month later, I was back in the same spot—holding those bottles of medication in my hand, knowing what I was about to do. This time, I didn't throw up. The pills went down, and I felt myself slipping away, sinking into a state where everything slowed down, like time itself was stopping.

I barely had the strength to move, but somehow, I managed to pull myself across the floor, dragging my body through the living room and into the kitchen. I knew I was home alone—that was the point—but something strange happened. The kitchen wasn't empty like I thought it would be.

There were people standing around small, round tables, dressed in club attire, like they had just come from a night out. They were looking at me, watching me like I was some kind of experiment, waiting to see what would happen. They didn't speak, didn't move—just stood there, staring. The whole scene was surreal, but it felt so real in that moment. I truly believed these people were there, watching me die.

Later, Justin would tell me that I had been alone in the house. **None of those people existed**, and the tables weren't even there. It was a near-death experience, probably a hallucination from the overdose, but at the time, I was convinced I had been surrounded by strangers, waiting for me to pass away.

I ended up back in the hospital, in the ICU once again, but this time, when I was released, Justin refused to take me back. I don't blame him. He had already tried to save me once, and now I was falling apart all over again. Instead of taking me back to his house, he dropped me off at a **mental health facility**, where I would spend the next 30 days.

The facility was sterile, cold, and unfamiliar. I was stuck there, processing everything that had led me to that point, and for the first time, I had to face the reality of my choices. I wasn't in Justin's chaotic, party-filled house anymore. I was in a place where all I had was time—time to think, time to confront my demons, and time to realize that something had to change.

CHAPTER 18

Running from Everything

When I first arrived at the mental health facility, I was exhausted. I had just tried to end my life, and my body and mind were completely drained. For days, I barely left my room. I slept endlessly, only coming out when I absolutely had to—for meds, meals, group sessions, and therapy. They forced me to participate, and while I wasn't in the mindset to engage, the routine kept me grounded. The facility was stark and sterile, a far cry from the chaotic life I'd been living with Justin.

I shared a room with a guy named **Jake**. He was there for the same reason as me—he had tried to end his life, too. His story was as chaotic as mine. He had a **crazy blonde girlfriend** who constantly talked down to him, pushing him deeper into his own trauma. He came from a broken home, a wrecked life, and in one moment of desperation, he stabbed through his entire wrist. When the cops arrived, he ran, bleeding out, until he passed out from exhaustion and blood loss. That's why he was there. During his time at the facility, he even tried reopening his stitches with a pencil, more than once.

That's the guy I was trapped in a room with for the night. But, as strange as it sounds, we became friends. We were both broken in our own ways, trying to make sense of a world that had pushed us to the edge. When we were released, it happened to be around the same time. Jake invited me to stay with him, and I accepted. It was his way of trying to be there for someone in the same darkness he was fighting through.

I went to live in the same house where Jake had tried to kill himself, a house filled with ghosts and bad memories. His girlfriend was still there—unstable, erratic—and the house itself was a place where they sold drugs. The room I was staying in didn't even have a door, just a thin barrier between me and the chaos that existed in the rest of the house. I was adjusting to new medications, trying to heal mentally, but the environment was anything but safe. It didn't take long for me to realize that if I stayed there, I would either end up dead or back in the hospital.

That's when **Liz** came into my life. I wasn't talking to my adopted parents at this point—they had cut me off completely, and I no longer existed to them. I had no one else, so I started looking for a roommate. I found Liz through an online ad, and she seemed willing to work with what I had. She arranged for me to be picked up from **Phoenix** and brought to her apartment in **Avondale, Arizona**.

When I arrived, I could tell right away something was off. Liz lived in a broken world, just like I did. The apartment was completely empty—no furniture, no food, no towels, nothing. The only thing in the whole place was a mattress on the floor that she shared with her little sister, who she was the guardian of. It was clear they came from a damaged background, but it didn't matter at the time. I needed somewhere to stay, and Liz was my only option.

There was an older couple living in the spare room at the time, but Liz kicked them out so I could move in. I used my **social security money** to furnish the place, buying rental furniture, getting us groceries, and trying to make the apartment livable. I even tried starting my own cam business, but the chaos of Liz's world began to close in around me. She became **possessive** quickly, not allowing me to leave and controlling how my money was spent. It didn't take long for me to see that she had her own secrets, and whatever they were, they created a toxic environment that suffocated me.

Liz had a friend across the hall named **Anna**, and I became close with her, but it didn't change the fact that everything about Liz felt off. We drank constantly, to the point of blacking out most nights. We smoked **synthetic marijuana**, which left us all brain-dead and disconnected from reality. It wasn't just the substances that were killing me—it was the control Liz had over my life. All of my money went to her, all of my decisions had to go through her. It became too much.

I knew, once again, that I had reached the edge. If I stayed, I would either die, end up in the ICU again, or worse. That's when I filed for my own apartment. To my surprise, I was approved. The apartment was on the third floor of a building a few blocks away from Liz's place. She was in **Building C**, and I was in **Building A**, which meant we wouldn't run into each other. I didn't tell her I was leaving. I waited until she was out with her sister, then I packed up my rental furniture and whatever else I had and moved out without saying a word.

The moment I stepped into my new apartment, it felt like heaven. For the first time in a long time, I had something that was mine. **Anna** and her boyfriend **Brian** were still my friends, and they would come over to party. We smoked **Spice**, drank hard liquor, watched movies, and tripped out, but even in this temporary relief, I could feel that something inside me still wasn't right.

Seven months passed, and I started feeling that familiar urge—the one to run. I knew if I stayed, I would destroy myself. I needed to escape, to start fresh somewhere far away from everything that had happened. That's when I grabbed a map, closed my eyes, and pointed.

I landed on **Galveston, Texas**.

Without telling anyone, I abandoned my apartment, leased a cheap car off Craigslist, and took off for the beach. I was running—running from my past, running from my probation, running from the life that was pulling me under. Galveston became my escape, the place where I hoped I could finally start over.

CHAPTER 19

Waves of Freedom and Chains of Betrayal

Driving into **Galveston** from **Houston** was like entering another world. The road stretched out in front of me, a straight path leading over a long bridge that seemed to go on forever. Galveston was an island, and as I drove over that bridge, the ocean came into view, the waves crashing against the shore. The sight of the ocean in front of me made me feel something I hadn't felt in a long time—**free**.

I pulled off the road before I reached the place I was going to stay. I had already arranged to rent a room from a strange old man who rented out every room in his house to different people, but before I got there, I needed a moment with the ocean. I parked the car, walked onto the beach, and stood there, letting the salt air fill my lungs. I watched the waves roll in and out, carrying my pain with them, pulling it away from me with each crash. For the first time in what felt like forever, I wasn't running from my past. I was standing still, looking at the vastness of the ocean, feeling small but **free**. The ocean has a way of putting everything in perspective—it shows you how insignificant your problems are compared to the vastness of the world.

After taking in the ocean, I drove further down the road and checked into the house where I'd be staying for the next few months. The man I rented the room from was odd, but I didn't care. I wasn't looking for stability, just a place to lay low. I was still drinking. Every day, I would grab a drink from the gas station, drive to the beach, and walk for hours, letting the world slip away behind me. It was my routine—a temporary escape from everything I had left behind.

After a few months, I found a **small condo** on the other side of the island. The landlord gave me a discount because of my disability, and it felt like another fresh start. I moved in, excited to finally have a place of my own. It was around this time that I met **Jim Greaser**, an older man who would come to mean a lot to me, though not in the way I expected. Jim and I started dating, and for a while, everything was good. He helped me fix up the condo, and we drank together almost every night. Jim was a bartender, and like many people I seemed to gravitate toward, he was a heavy drinker. There was a comfort in that, a familiarity. It's strange how we're drawn to the same patterns, even when we know they're toxic.

For a time, it felt like I was building something. I had even started a new career, something I never expected. I stumbled across **Bitwine**, an online network for psychic readings. I signed up under a stage name to keep my identity private, and it turned out I was good—really good. Clients started coming in, one after the other, and soon I was making over $5,000 a month. For someone like me, that was life-changing money. I bought myself a **black Firebird t-top**, a car I loved. Driving it made me feel like **Batman**, like I was untouchable. For the first time, I was creating something for myself.

But as always, the good times didn't last.

One afternoon, I was making a pot of spaghetti in my condo when there was a knock at the door. I didn't think much of it, blindly opening the door without any sense of what was waiting for me on the other side. **Several cops** were standing there, with more waiting at the back door. My heart sank. They had found me. The **run was over**.

I was arrested and booked into the **Galveston jail**. I lost everything in that moment—**the condo**, my **car**, all the nice furniture I had bought, even my **cat**. Everything I had built up during my time in Galveston was gone in an instant. And the person responsible? **Jim**.

I didn't find out until later, but Jim had turned me in. He had arranged the whole thing, using the excuse that he knew I would never turn myself in, and in a way, he was right. I wasn't ready to face my past. I wasn't ready for the certainty of **jail time**. At first, I was furious. But after some time, I realized he had done me a favor. I couldn't keep running forever.

What hurt more than being turned in was what Jim did while I was in jail. He convinced me to sign over **power of attorney** to him, claiming it was to support me while I was locked up. I trusted him, and it was a mistake. Over the next nine months, while I sat in that Galveston jail waiting for **Arizona** to come get me, Jim drained my bank account. He took everything I had, and eventually, he stopped taking my calls. He stopped writing back. He abandoned me like so many others had before.

After nine months, **Arizona** finally came to pick me up. The ride back was a grueling three-day journey, cramped in a van, handcuffed at the wrists and ankles, packed in with other inmates being transported across state lines. But as exhausting as it was, there was a strange sense of relief when I was finally booked into the **Safford jail**.

Being back in **Arizona**, facing the problems I had run from, felt like the start of something different. There was a sense of peace in finally confronting the mess I had made of my life. But even though I was so close to the people who had raised me—**Terry** and **Teresa**—they still wouldn't take my calls. Out of the dozens of letters I sent, they only replied to two. Once again, I was left to face the consequences of my choices alone.

CHAPTER 20

Returning to Familiar Chaos

Coming back to **Arizona** after those few years on the run felt strangely comforting. After all the chaos in **Galveston**, returning to the state where everything had started gave me a sense of relief. I wasn't running anymore. I didn't have to hide or look over my shoulder. I was finally facing the problems I had tried so hard to escape. Though it wasn't by choice, I was beginning to make things right.

While I was in **Safford jail**, I met a man named **Andy**. He was gay, like me, and we bonded over that. In jail, having someone who understood that part of me was rare, and we grew close quickly. Eventually, we ended up in the same pod, and that's when I found out Andy had a boyfriend—an older man named **Mario**. Mario would write to Andy daily, and it was clear how much he cared for him. I couldn't help but feel jealous. I was going to get out soon, but I had nowhere to go, while Andy had this devoted man waiting for him.

That's when my **survival mode** kicked in. I knew I needed a plan, and I saw an opening. **Behind Andy's back**, I wrote to Mario. I didn't expect much, but to my surprise, he responded. We exchanged letters, and a connection started to form. Andy eventually found out about it, and he was furious. He called me across the pod one day, and I knew we were going to fight. He asked me straight-up if I had been talking to his boyfriend, and I told him the truth—**yes**. I braced myself for a punch, but instead, Andy turned and punched the guy standing next to him in the mouth. The poor guy started bleeding, and Andy ended up getting moved into isolation for the incident.

With Andy out of the way, I kept writing to Mario, and things escalated. **Mario** started visiting me in jail, and it didn't take long before he **fell in love with me**, or at least what he thought was love. I knew it wasn't real love—I didn't even find him attractive. He was older, grotesque, and clearly addicted to meth, but I played the part because I needed somewhere to go once I was released.

When I finally got out on house arrest, **Mario's house** was where I went. I stayed in his extra bedroom, trying to make the best of it. What I didn't know at the time was how deep Mario's addiction ran. He was a full-blown meth addict, and it wasn't long before he pulled me back into that world. The day I was released, I celebrated by getting a big bottle of vodka, a pack of cigarettes, and a computer. I got drunk and went back to work on **Bitwine**, the psychic reading platform I had been using before.

Bitwine was going well, but I wanted more. That's when I found **Kasamba**, a more high-end psychic reading network. It was formerly known as **LivePerson**, but had since branched off into a dedicated psychic site. I started making **real money** there, up to ten thousand dollars a month. For someone like me, that was a dream come true. I used the money to rent a small apartment and finally moved out of Mario's house. I knew I couldn't stay with him forever—he was **a psychopath**, and being around him would have led to disaster.

Once I was out of Mario's house, things began to pick up career-wise. I was making up to **thirty thousand dollars a month** at one point, and with that money, I managed to rent-to-own a **new two-bedroom house** from a doctor. It felt like I had finally built the life I had been chasing—financial security, a beautiful house, and the freedom to work on my terms. But as always, the darkness was never far behind.

During this time, **Hope** came back into my life. She had changed drastically. She had fallen deeper into addiction and was now using **oxy pills**, which she smoked like heroin. She had a daughter during this time, a child who was born addicted to drugs and was taken away by the state. Her life was a mess, and in some ways, so was mine. I was still doing **meth**, still smoking **Spice**, and still drinking heavily. The only difference was that I had money now, but that didn't change the fact that I was falling apart.

Hope started coming over to my two-story house all the time. She would get high and do her makeup in my bathroom, and sometimes her boyfriend **Sam** would come over too. Sam wasn't worried about me being around—he knew I was gay, and even though I still loved Hope, it wasn't in a romantic way anymore. We had been through too much together for that.

But Hope was using me. She would borrow money, borrow my car, and I knew I was being taken advantage of. That's what happens when you're around addicts—it takes one to know one. You get sucked into a cycle of using each other, and we were no different.

During this time, I reconnected with **Teresa** and **Terry**. Things had changed between us. **Terry** was distant, more so than ever before, and I can't say I blamed him. **Teresa**, on the other hand, seemed more welcoming, like she was finally ready to let me back into their lives. But I knew why—she had already won. **Caleb** was hers now, and she had no reason to fight me anymore. Caleb saw them as his parents, he called Teresa "mom," and I was just **T.J.** to him, not his dad. Even though my legal name was **Derrick Bullock** by this time, to Caleb, I was always **T.J.**, and that's how it would stay.

I knew I had lost. Caleb was fully theirs, and there was nothing I could do to change that. I had to accept it. Teresa and Terry still had a power over me, a judgmental presence that I felt every time I was around them, even if they didn't say anything directly. It was in the way they looked at me, the way they talked about Caleb. They had taken him away, and I had no choice but to play the part they wanted me to play—**the outsider** in my own son's life.

As the months passed, **Hope** kept coming around, using me more and more. But I didn't care. I was falling back into old habits, doing meth, drinking, and continuing to spiral, all while hiding it from my probation officers. I had gotten good at hiding my addictions. I was too cunning, too charming to get caught, and I always found a way to make it through without facing the consequences. But deep down, I knew it was only a matter of time before it all caught up to me.

CHAPTER 21

Spiraling and New Beginnings

I knew things were spiraling out of control when the money stopped coming in. My once-successful psychic career on **Kasamba** and **Bitwine** began to dwindle, and I found myself working less and less. The days of making thousands of dollars each month were behind me. It was subtle at first—just a slow decline. But soon, the money dried up completely, and I was left facing the consequences of my addiction, my impulsive decisions, and my chaotic lifestyle.

Eventually, I could no longer afford the **two-story home** I had been renting to own. It was a house I had poured so much into, hoping it would be the foundation for a stable life, but I had lost that battle again. I was forced to move out, and the only place left to go was my **Grandma Turner's old doublewide trailer**. It had been sitting vacant for a while, and I figured I would just **buy it** and live the rest of my life there.

I cleaned it out, moved in, and tried to convince myself that everything was okay. But deep down, I knew I had failed. The money was gone, and I was back at square one. **Terry and Teresa** weren't dumb—they probably knew what had happened. But I kept up the facade, pretending that everything was fine, even though the reality was anything but.

It was at that trailer, in my lowest moments, that I met a man online. His name was **Ivan**, and he was from **New Mexico**. He was black, and something about him drew me in quickly. He was my way out of a bad situation, someone who didn't know my past, someone who hadn't had time to learn to dislike me yet. He was a new beginning, or so I thought.

Ivan was passing through Arizona on some trip, and we arranged to meet. I picked him up from a nearby town where his bus had dropped him off and brought him back to my trailer in **Safford**. We spent a few days together, getting to know each other. I fell for him fast. He invited me to move with him to **New Mexico**, and I didn't hesitate. It was another escape—another chance to start over.

Ivan didn't have his own place; he lived with his **aunt and uncle**, and that's where we stayed for the first few weeks until we found a rental in **Santa Fe**. It felt like I was on the verge of something new again. But the cracks in the relationship started to show almost immediately.

My drinking had gotten out of control by then. I was lost in the bottle, and though I tried to ignore the signs, I knew **Ivan** was cheating on me. It wasn't even subtle. He would disappear for hours, sometimes days, and there was always a tension between us. Our sex life was practically nonexistent. Like every other relationship I'd been in, we ended up in **separate rooms**, living like roommates instead of lovers.

One night, I tried to go down on Ivan, and the taste told me everything I needed to know. His junk tasted like **shit**—fresh shit—and I knew it wasn't mine. That was the confirmation I had been avoiding. Ivan was cheating on me, and he didn't even care to hide it. My suspicions were confirmed when I met the man Ivan had been cheating with—**Anthony**.

Anthony had been in a relationship with Ivan for over a year, long before I ever came into the picture. The worst part was that Anthony knew about me before I even knew about him. Ivan had been playing both sides, and I was just another piece in his game.

After I broke up with Ivan, he continued to torment me. Like the creep he was, he rented the house **next door** to mine. We had to share the same driveway, parking our cars side by side, even though we were no longer together. It was maddening, but it was also the moment that would change everything.

Ivan went out of town one night—probably to meet another guy—and **Anthony** was left house-sitting for him. I had **Jannette**, one of Anthony's old roommates, staying with me at the time. That night, Anthony got drunk, and he needed a **corkscrew** to open his bottle. Jannette was going to take it over to him, but being the diva I am, I told her to let me do it. I walked over to Ivan's house, corkscrew in hand, and that's when **Anthony** and I clicked.

I invited him over to do karaoke with Jannette and me. He accepted, and that night, the three of us drank, laughed, and sang together. For the first time in what felt like ages, I felt at peace. **Anthony** was my kind of people. We clicked instantly, and from that moment on, I never let him leave my side.

While Ivan was still out of town, Anthony helped me take back the things Ivan had stolen from me—clothes, furniture, anything that was mine. We bonded over that shared sense of reclaiming what was rightfully mine, and when Ivan returned, I was already done with him. Anthony moved in with me, and that was the start of something I didn't expect—a **long, beautiful, and complicated relationship** that would become the most significant of my life.

CHAPTER 22

A Love Built in Chaos

When **Anthony** moved in, we became close fast. We had so much in common—drinking, partying, and a shared sense of running from the past. We bonded over our love for **sushi** and alcohol. I know it sounds reckless, and in many ways, it was, but that was my mentality at the time. We were living for the moment, burying everything else underneath a haze of alcohol and indulgence.

Early on, Anthony worked at the same hospital where **Ivan** worked, which made things complicated. Ivan still hadn't let go of the past, and there were times when Anthony and I didn't feel safe even leaving the house. Ivan was constantly lurking, causing tension and making us feel like we had to record everything just in case something happened. It was suffocating.

One night, Anthony told me he had **$1.5k** in his bank account and didn't know how to spend it. Me being me, I told him I could help with that. We spent it all on sushi and alcohol, having the time of our lives, as if there were no consequences. And for a while, there weren't. Anthony managed to keep his job, but I eventually convinced him to **quit**. I couldn't stand the idea of him working in the same place as Ivan, and the paranoia I felt at the time was eating me alive.

We needed to get out of there. **Anthony's older brother, Eric**, stepped in and helped us find a place—a beautiful **farmhouse** outside of **Las Vegas, New Mexico**, where Anthony's whole family lived. The ranch land stretched out for miles, and everyone was within about a mile of one another. It was peaceful, isolated, and it felt like a fresh start. Anthony secured a job at a **nursing home** in Las Vegas, where he would end up working for a few years.

The farmhouse became our sanctuary, a place where we could escape from the world and from Ivan's constant shadow. But despite the peace of the land, we were still **alcoholics**. My life revolved around **Spice**, alcohol, and my social security checks. Anthony's income went mostly to our addictions. I was still a mess, still mentally unstable, but instead of facing it, I buried it deeper, hiding behind the routine of our life in New Mexico.

After years of dealing with legal issues, I finally got **released from Arizona probation**. It was a relief to have that weight lifted, but the freedom didn't last long. The problems were far from over. Our relationship was volatile. The drinking fueled **physical fights** between us, and my paranoia about Anthony cheating only made things worse. I had never trusted men, and every time I thought about it, the old wounds reopened.

One night, after Anthony came home from work, I was convinced he was cheating on me. I had no proof, but that didn't matter. My insecurities took control. I confronted him, and things escalated fast. In a moment of blind rage, I **hit him in the nose**. Blood poured down his face, and before I knew it, his brother **Eric** was at the house. Eric saw the blood and immediately assumed the worst. I lied, saying someone had hit Anthony at work, but no one believed me—not even myself.

Eric was furious. He **tackled me to the ground**, pinning me down and unleashing a barrage of punches to my face and head. I pushed him off, desperate to defend myself, and grabbed a **fake stage prop knife** that Anthony had as a gift. It wasn't real, but in the heat of the moment, I ran at Eric with it. The knife wasn't going to do anything, but Eric didn't know that. He sprinted for his truck, grabbed a gun, and fired a few rounds into the air. Things were out of control.

That's when **Anthony's family** stepped in. They called the cops, and the **New Mexico State Police** arrived since we were so far out from town. They took me in, and I ended up spending **30 days in jail**. During that time, Anthony's family tried to convince him to leave me. They packed up his things and tried to haul him away while I was locked up. They had every right to—they were a protective family, and they saw me as a threat to their son. They were only trying to save him.

But **Anthony stayed**.

He saw something in me that the others didn't. By then, I had already shared much of my life with him, and we had begun to connect on a deeper level. He saw past the rage, the addiction, and the chaos. He saw the brokenness that was hiding underneath all of it. **We were falling in love**, but not the kind of love that comes from lust or excitement. This was the real kind of love, the kind I had never experienced before—the kind that was built on understanding and compassion.

When I got out of jail, Anthony was there waiting for me. His family couldn't believe it. They had wanted him to move on, to leave me in the past, but he refused. He loved me in a way no one else ever had. He stood by me when everyone else would have walked away. He saw the parts of me that I didn't even know how to love myself.

At the time, I didn't fully realize it, but Anthony would become the **one person on the planet I could trust**, the one person who saw me for who I really was and still chose to stay. We were both flawed, both broken in different ways, but together, we found something worth fighting for.

CHAPTER 23

A Toxic Love in the Desert

I wish I could say that the first time I went to jail for hitting **Anthony** was the last, but it wasn't. **Our love was real**, but it was also **toxic**, and every time I drank, all the pain, anger, and hurt that I kept buried inside would find its way out. I'd hurt the one person I loved most in the world. I couldn't control it, and **Anthony** was always on the receiving end.

To no one's surprise, I ended up back on **probation**, a cycle that would continue for the next few years. But even with all the drinking, fighting, and chaos, **Anthony loved me anyway**. He had his own battle scars, his own trauma, and we bonded over the fact that we were both broken in different ways. It wasn't perfect, far from it, but we held on to each other because, deep down, we knew we were all the other had.

Living out on **Eric's ranch** was both a blessing and a curse. It was quiet, and for a while, it felt like a sanctuary. We were surrounded by **animals**, and Eric had everything—a ton of dogs from his breeding business, **horses, goats, pigs**, and whatever else he could take care of. Early in the mornings, we'd wake up around **5:30 AM**, already drunk from the night before or cracking open another bottle to start the day, and head over to Eric's house to help him with the animals.

There was something oddly satisfying about it. We'd **rake up the animal poop**, feed the animals, clean the kennels—it was hard work, but when you're drunk, it doesn't feel that way. It was a bizarre mix of **fun** and **self-destruction**, but for us, it worked.

Anthony had started working at the **nursing home** in **Las Vegas**, NM, and things seemed to be stabilizing a bit, at least financially. But there was still tension with Eric. We'd been working off a deal with him to **lease a red car** in exchange for helping with the farm work, but one day, everything fell apart.

It was **Anthony's first day** at the nursing home, and I just wanted to stay home. **I didn't show up** to help Eric that morning, and by the end of the day, Eric had taken back the red car. I didn't understand it at the time, but looking back, I wonder if it was still because of what had happened between **Anthony and me**, the fight, the lies, the bloody nose. Maybe Eric still held a grudge.

Despite that setback, Anthony and I were doing our best to move forward. Things shifted when a **lesbian couple** showed interest in buying the ranch house we were living in, and we had no choice but to **move out**. It wasn't a situation we could control, but it pushed us to the next chapter in our lives.

We found a **singlewide trailer** in a mobile home park in Las Vegas. The home belonged to **Anthony's dad**, but a woman was living there who hadn't been paying rent for months. She owed thousands in back payments and was being evicted by the court. When she was finally gone, we had to get a **locksmith** to open the door, and what we found inside was horrific.

The floors were covered in about an inch of **dog poop, trash, and filth**. The entire trailer was a disaster. But it was ours now, and we had to clean it out. We pulled up the floors, replaced them, painted the walls, brought in new appliances, and put up new skirting on the outside. By the time we were done, the trailer looked brand new, and we had made it **home**.

It was finally something that felt permanent, something no one could take away from us. By this time, we already had **Jacky**, our first dog together. She was a small, tan, short-haired chihuahua with a pink nose, and she was everything to us. It was **me, Anthony, and Jacky against the world**. We had built a life together, one full of struggle and pain, but also love. I could feel us **falling deeper in love** with each other, even through all the chaos.

We had finally found a rhythm. But one day, there was a knock at the door. It was **Anthony's niece** and her then-girlfriend. They were crying, and the news they brought hit us like a ton of bricks: **Eric was in the hospital**—in **critical condition**.

CHAPTER 24

Death, Grief, and a Golden UFO

By the time **Eric** passed away, Anthony and I had been together for about three years. We had built a small family of our own, with our three dogs—**Jacky, Pebbles**, and **Billy**—who meant everything to us. **Jacky** was our oldest, the little tan chihuahua with a pink nose who had been with us from the start. Then there was **Pebbles**, a small black dog that looked like a poodle but wasn't, a bit bigger than Jacky. Finally, we had **Billy**, our little black shitzu who was short, fat, and loved food more than anything. Billy was a handful. I'll never forget the time she swallowed a whole meatball without even chewing it. She started **choking**, and I had to do the **Heimlich maneuver** to save her. To this day, I still have PTSD from that moment.

Life had become a strange mix of love, chaos, and survival. **Anthony and I still fought**, just like we always had. We drank heavily—daily, in fact—and when we drank, the blackouts came. It wasn't unusual for one of us to wake up with a new injury from the night before. One morning, **Anthony woke up with a black eye**, and we both knew it had been another one of those nights where we hurt each other in ways we didn't even remember.

That morning, the **knock on the door** came. It was **Brittany**, Anthony's niece—**Patricia's** daughter. She was with her girlfriend at the time, and the news she brought shook our world to its core.

"**Eric shot himself in the head**," she said, her voice shaky. "They're taking him to the hospital."

Anthony sat there in shock, and I could barely process it. As Brittany and her girlfriend rushed to the hospital, I told Anthony what had happened. He was still trying to pull himself together, still trying to hide the bruises from our fight. He **covered his black eye** with concealer, and we made our way to the hospital, hearts pounding, fear gripping us both.

By the time we arrived, **Eric had already passed away**. Anthony's mom and dad were there, as were most of the family members who could make it in time, except for **Eric's wife**, who didn't show up until hours later. The hospital was heavy with grief, the air thick with disbelief. Eric, who had been such a central figure in Anthony's life, was gone. Just like that.

There are moments in life that you can never fully explain, things that don't fit into the logical world we know. As we left the hospital, **something incredible happened**. We were driving back home, the weight of Eric's death hanging over us, when we both looked up at the sky above **Stormie Lake**, not far from the hospital.

There, in the sky, was a **golden, egg-shaped UFO**. It was just sitting there, motionless, glowing above the lake. We both saw it, clear as day, and in that moment, we knew what it was. To us, it wasn't just a UFO—it was **Eric**, or at least his spirit, being taken home by his spirit family. It was a bizarre, otherworldly confirmation that his soul had moved on.

Anthony cried that night, something he rarely ever did. But even in his grief, he didn't fully process it. Like me, **he buried it deep**. He didn't talk about his feelings, didn't express the hurt. He just pushed it down, pretended it didn't exist, and went on with life. I, on the other hand, was the opposite. **I couldn't stop talking about my feelings**, and in some ways, I think it drove us both crazy. I had no filters, no boundaries, and I would spill my emotions out whenever they rose to the surface.

But we were both struggling, both trying to move on in our own ways. We **drowned ourselves in liquor**, trying to fill the gaping hole left by Eric's death. It wasn't the healthiest way to cope, but it was the only way we knew how. **Anthony never fully grieved**, and even today, I don't think he ever allowed himself to feel the full weight of losing his brother. It was just another wound he buried beneath the surface.

Amidst all this pain and turmoil, something unexpected happened. It was during this time that I started working on **Fiverr** as an online psychic. I already had the **gifts**. I already had the **expertise**. I knew how to do psychic readings, and for years I had been honing those abilities. But I didn't think much of it when I set up my account. It was just a side hobby, something to pass the time.

But **Fiverr** took off in a big way. It was the **one good thing** to come out of that dark period. What started as a side gig quickly turned into a full-fledged career. I began getting client after client, building a name for myself in the online psychic world. It was a strange kind of silver lining in the midst of all the chaos, but it gave me something to focus on, something to pour my energy into when everything else felt like it was falling apart.

Anthony was still working at the **nursing home**, but as my Fiverr business grew, I began to see a path forward, a way to build something for us. And though we were still broken, still drinking, still fighting, there was a glimmer of hope in that small success.

CHAPTER 25

Success, Strain, and the Return of My Sister

By the time I hit **31**, things were changing rapidly. **Anthony** and I had been together for four years by then, and I had started working on **Fiverr** as an online psychic. The decision to do psychic readings under a stage name wasn't just a professional choice—it was about **protecting myself and Anthony**. Our safety mattered more than anything, and I didn't want people from my past finding me or meddling in our lives. I needed to keep my private life separate from my professional one.

I worked from home, which was already challenging in itself. But it didn't take long before Fiverr became wildly successful. Within just **five months**, I was making enough money that **Anthony was able to quit his job** at the nursing home and come home full-time. At first, it felt like a victory. The thought of us being together 24/7 seemed perfect at the time—like we were getting everything we had wanted. But it turned out to be much harder than we anticipated.

When you're suddenly **together all the time**, without breaks, it tests a relationship in ways you don't expect. We started to feel the effects of **cabin fever**, and when **COVID-19** hit, it only made things worse. The lockdowns, the isolation from the world, and the pressure of being constantly in each other's space—it was suffocating at times. We had already been through so much together, but this was a new kind of challenge, one that neither of us was fully prepared for.

And just when I thought things couldn't get any crazier, **Tasha** came back into my life.

My **biological sister** had been in **prison in Arizona** for ten years on **drug charges, forgery**, and God knows what else. We had only spoken on the phone since I was a child, and the idea of having her back in my life seemed like a way to **fill the void**. She had been my original best friend, my family before everything fell apart, and I wanted to believe that this would be a new chapter for us—a chapter of healing and reconnection.

So, I arranged everything for her release. I handled her **plane ticket** to **New Mexico**, booked a **hotel** for her to stay in the night before, and picked her up from the airport the next day. This was all during the height of the pandemic, so it was a stressful and scary time. But I made it happen because I believed in second chances, and I thought we could rebuild our bond.

Tasha moved into our already small singlewide trailer, which was cramped with **three dogs** and now the addition of another person. It was exciting at first, though. I felt something I hadn't felt in years—**complete**. I had my sister back. I had Anthony, the man I loved. I had built a career that allowed me to support us all. For the first time, it felt like the pieces of my life were coming together.

At least, that's what I told myself.

But when someone has been a **hardcore criminal** their entire life, fresh out of a **decade in prison**, they're not going to be the person you hope they will be. And Tasha, as much as I wanted to believe in her, was far from the person I had imagined she would be.

The problems started small. **Tasha wasn't adjusting** to life outside of prison the way I hoped. She brought a certain chaos with her, a darkness that I hadn't seen in years. At first, I tried to rationalize it. She had been through a lot, and it would take time for her to adjust to a new life. But as the days went on, it became clear that **her problems weren't going to go away**.

Her attitude, her actions, the way she treated both **Anthony and me**—it was becoming too much. She was **manipulative** and still carried the criminal mindset that had gotten her into prison in the first place. I tried to make excuses for her, telling myself it was just the stress of her new freedom. But deep down, I knew better.

Anthony saw it too, though he was more patient about it than I was. But there were cracks forming—between me and Tasha, between me and Anthony. I had brought her into our home, thinking I was doing the right thing, thinking that this was my chance to finally have my family back. But instead of **healing**, it felt like the past was repeating itself.

I started to realize that, despite all my best intentions, **some people don't change**. No matter how much you want them to, no matter how much you try to help, some people are stuck in their ways. Tasha wasn't the sister I remembered from childhood. She wasn't my "best friend" anymore. She was someone I barely knew—someone with a history of lies, manipulation, and chaos.

It wasn't long before I started to regret even reaching out to her.

And yet, for a while, I **tried to ignore the signs**. I wanted to believe that we could make it work, that we could be a family again. But the truth was, I had brought someone into my home who didn't have my best interests at heart. And it wasn't just hurting me—it was hurting Anthony, too.

Even with all of this going on, the **success of my Fiverr career** was booming. I was making more money than ever, and while that should have felt like a victory, it only added more pressure. **Anthony and I** were home all day, every day, with nothing but time to **drink, fight, and try to figure out how to make this new life work**. We had already been struggling with cabin fever, and adding Tasha to the mix was like throwing gasoline on a fire.

CHAPTER 26

A Betrayal, a Goodbye, and a New Beginning

By the time **Tasha** moved in with us, I was **33 years old**, still caught in a cycle of heavy drinking. The days bled into nights, and I was waking up every day only to **drink until I passed out** again. That was my reality. I was stressed, though I never admitted it to myself. Alcohol was my coping mechanism, the thing that allowed me to push everything down, to ignore the pain and chaos in my life. It was easier to drown it than to face it.

Tasha wasn't any better. In many ways, she was worse. **Fresh out of prison** after a decade inside, she wasn't adjusting to life on the outside. The three of us—**Anthony, Tasha**, and I—drank heavily every day, and the tension in the house was growing. I had expected to have my sister back, my **original best friend**, but instead, she was stirring up trouble behind my back.

When **Anthony and Tasha** would go to the store, **Anthony** would tell me how she talked behind my back, questioning how he "puts up with me." She would say things like, "I could never do it." To my face, Tasha was **sweet**. She called me **"bubba"**, acting like everything was fine between us. But behind my back, she was manipulating the situation, playing us both.

The signs were there early on—**Tasha hoarding food**, hiding it in her room like she was still in prison. She acted like Anthony's new car, which I had just bought for him, was hers to use. She'd take it without asking, and there was this sense of entitlement in her actions. But I let it go because she was my sister. I thought I owed her that much. After all, I had spent my whole life wanting a family, and now that I had her back, I was determined to make it work. Even if it meant ignoring the warning signs.

But that all changed one night.

Anthony had already passed out in his bed, and I was drunk, almost **blacked out** myself. I wandered into **Tasha's room** to chill, talk, and vibe, just as we had many times before. The conversation shifted to **Anthony**, though I can't remember how or why. And then, out of nowhere, **Tasha leaned in to kiss me**.

This wasn't a sibling kiss. It wasn't innocent. She was crossing a line, and it shattered any illusion I had of rebuilding a normal relationship with her. **Tasha told me she could be Anthony's and my surrogate**, that she could carry a child for us. It was sick, twisted, and completely out of line.

I froze. In that moment, everything changed. I felt **broken**. This was my **biological sister**, someone I had spent my entire life wishing to be close to, someone I thought I could trust. And she had crossed a boundary I never thought would be tested. **How could I ever see her the same way?**

The next morning, **Anthony and I packed up and left**. We needed to get away. We spent a week in **Carlsbad** and **Roswell**, just trying to process what had happened. I couldn't be in that house with her anymore. We left **Tasha** to watch the dogs while we were gone, but when we got back, I knew I couldn't let her stay.

She left to visit her girlfriend in Arizona, and while she was gone, I sent her a message. I told her she wasn't **welcome to come back**. I made up an excuse about **COVID**, saying that because she was out going to **casinos** and other public places, she was a risk to us. But the real reason was what she had done to me that night. I couldn't live under the same roof as her anymore.

That was the end of it. I haven't seen **Tasha** since that day. She went back to Arizona, and from what I've read online, she ended up back in **jail** for **drugs, burglary**, and God knows what else. The sister I had dreamed of reconnecting with was gone, and in her place was just another person from my past, someone who had hurt me in ways I couldn't forget. I don't regret cutting her out of my life. That **connection is dead**, and I have no intention of ever seeing her again.

But the hits didn't stop there. Shortly after cutting ties with **Tasha**, I got a message from my **father**.

I had always wondered about him. He found me through an **ancestry DNA website**, and after some back and forth, we connected on **Facebook**. We started texting and talking, though there was always an underlying anger in me. How could he have **given me up** when I was two? How could he have just signed me over like I was nothing?

He told me it wasn't him. He said his **brother**, who had the same name—**Johnny Clifton Robinson**—had signed the papers. He wanted me to believe it, and for a while, I did. But I had the documents, and **his name was right there**, clear as day. It was him. He had signed me away.

Two days before my **35th birthday**, on **October 5th**, my father passed away from **heart complications** and **dementia**. He died just before my birthday, and to this day, I still feel like that was his final betrayal. The last thing he told me was a lie. I found out from his **obituary** that it was, in fact, **him** who had signed me away. He had lied to me, and then he died before I had the chance to confront him about it.

I regret not being kinder to him, not giving him more of a chance, but the anger was there. I was hurt. And I'll never get the answers I needed from him. I'll never get closure. Now, my fear is that **Caleb** will do the same to me. That he'll grow up and resent me, that he'll have the same anger I had toward my father. It's a **cycle**—one that I fear will continue until someone breaks it.

Amidst all of this pain, Anthony and I made one of the most important decisions of our lives. We **bought a house**, in the same town, but this time it was a real home—a place we could call ours. It was an **actual house**, not a trailer. It was a fresh start, and we've lived there for the past **four years**, surrounded by our **eight dogs**. It's the life we've built together, despite everything we've been through.

CHAPTER 27

A New Home, A New Life

When I kicked **Tasha** out of my life, I didn't just lose a sister—I gained a new sense of peace. But more than that, I gained another family member: **Raina**, the puppy I had originally gotten for Tasha. It was clear from the beginning that **Raina never liked her**. Dogs can sense things in people, things we might not want to see or admit. And Raina sensed something dark in Tasha. After she left, Raina stayed, and she became one of the pack.

To this day, **Raina** is still with us, living here in our new home. She's grown into a beautiful dog, always attached to **Anthony**, as if she knew from the start who her real family was.

Our pack of dogs has grown since those days. **Blanca**—my spirit dog—has been by my side through it all. Then there's **Charlie**, our short-legged dachshund-like pup who everyone falls in love with. **Chelsea** and **Chandler** are the siblings. **Chandler**, the runt of the litter, had to be **bottle-fed** by Anthony when he was just a baby, and now, even though he's two years old, he still acts like a puppy.

Having **eight dogs** is a challenge, to say the least. **All of them are indoor dogs**, and at times it can be overwhelming. When I'm working at my computer, trying to write or do psychic readings, it's hard to concentrate with a dog jumping on or off me every few minutes. It's constant. Sometimes I can barely type a few lines before I'm interrupted by one of the dogs needing attention. But that's part of the life we've built.

Despite the chaos, there's nothing better than waking up to being **tackled by kisses** and feeling surrounded by love. That's what our home has become: a place filled with unconditional love. **Anthony** and the dogs are my entire world. They're my family. I don't have friends outside of them. I don't need them. **Anthony** is the only person I love, the only person I trust, the only friend I have. Outside of my clients on **Fiverr**, I don't talk to anyone else.

But that's okay. **We've built a life** that suits us, one that is financially secure and emotionally fulfilling. I still work under my **professional name** on Fiverr, and I've kept my two lives—personal and professional—strictly separate. In my professional life, I've written **several books**, but none of them fulfilled me the way I thought they would. There was always something missing, something I couldn't quite put my finger on.

That's why I'm here today, writing this book. I'm trying to find **myself** again. The **real me**, not just the person I've become under my work name. As much as I love the success I've found as a psychic, as much as I enjoy the work side of me, there's still a part of me that needs to reconnect with my true identity.

That's why this book is so important. It's about reclaiming who I am, about showing the world the person behind the stage name. It's about being **Derrick Caleb Solano**—the man who has survived everything life has thrown at him, the man who refuses to break.

Anthony and I married back when we still lived in that trailer. **April 28th, 2018**—the day I took his name and became **Derrick Caleb Solano**. We've been legally married for over **six years**, but we've been together for **over a decade** now. In those years, so much has changed. We've both stopped drinking. We've stopped fighting. The toxic cycles that once dominated our relationship have disappeared, and we're both **thriving** in ways we never thought possible.

Anthony works out now, getting stronger both physically and mentally, and I'm sitting here writing this book—something I never thought I'd have the strength or clarity to do. We've both grown so much, and we've left behind the darker parts of our past.

And now, I've written a **song** to pair with this book. It's called **"I Won't Break,"** and it's my declaration to the world, a reflection of everything I've been through and the unbreakable spirit that I've discovered within myself. This song, like this book, is a testament to **survival**. It's a celebration of the life Anthony and I have built together, the love we've fought to protect, and the peace we've finally earned.

Life isn't perfect, but it's **coming together**. After years of trauma, addiction, betrayal, and loss, we've found a place where we can breathe, a place we can call our own. And none of it would have been possible without Anthony's belief in me, his **unconditional love**, and the **family** we've created together—with our dogs, our home, and the life we've built side by side.

We've finally earned the love, the break, and the **security** we've always deserved.

CHAPTER 28

The Shadows of the Past

No matter how much you think you've escaped it, **the past always catches up with you**. Even now, after **Anthony** and I have built this life of **security**, the ghosts of what came before still creep into the present. One of those ghosts was a decision I made when I first got approved for **disability**.

Back then, everything was still fresh. **Caleb** had just been taken from me, and I still believed I was going to get him back. So when I was filing for **social security**, I claimed him as a **dependent**. At the time, I didn't think twice about it. It made sense—I was his father. Even though I wasn't physically raising him, I felt entitled to that status because I thought he would come home to me one day.

For years, this went unnoticed. I was getting **social security** checks every month, well into my thirties, with a small additional amount for **Caleb**. I should've known that something like that wouldn't go unchecked forever, but I never considered the consequences. I had so many other things on my plate, emotionally and mentally, that I barely thought about the money.

Then, out of nowhere, it caught up with me. They cut me off from **social security**, and I was told I had to **repay $79,000**. And all at once. I couldn't believe it. How had it slipped through the cracks for so many years? And why, of all times, was it coming back to bite me now?

A part of me still believes **Teresa** had something to do with it. Maybe it's paranoia, but she's always had ways of getting what she wants, and she's never stopped trying to control the situation with Caleb. Regardless of how it happened, the debt was there. I had to face it.

But in a strange way, I found some **comfort** in it. At least that money went to Caleb. At least he got something out of it. When I saw his **Instagram** and **Facebook** posts earlier this year, after he turned **18** in **June 2024**, I saw him with his new car—a white one. And in my heart, I hope that money helped him buy it. Maybe, in some way, I was still able to contribute to his life, even if I wasn't a part of it.

The truth is, I haven't spoken to **Caleb** in years. I don't have contact with him, and I don't push it. I want to give him his **space**. After all these years, I'm sure **Teresa** has fed him the narrative that I'm just some loser, an addict who abandoned him. It's what she's always thought of me, and I can only imagine how she's painted me in his eyes.

The last time I saw Caleb was on **Labor Day**, many years ago. **Anthony** and I had driven to **their town** to visit. We were staying at a hotel nearby, one with a pool, and we invited Caleb to come swim with us. **Teresa** had to come too, of course—there was no way she was going to let him be with us alone. And when we asked if Caleb could ride with us in the car, the answer was an immediate "**no**." She still thought we would **steal him**, even then.

That whole visit was filled with tension. Teresa kept talking about how **Terry's family**—the same family that lived in the area—**hated me** because of that $300 I borrowed years ago. She made it clear that I wasn't welcome, and I was better off staying away. That was the last time I saw Caleb in person, the last time I had any interaction with the **Richins family**. That was at least six to eight years ago.

Now, I'm at the point where I know it's better to **stay away**. If Caleb ever wants to find me, that's his choice. I won't push myself into his life. Nothing that happened was his fault, and I don't want to mess up his life in any way. I just hope, deep down, that he finds his own version of the truth someday.

Aside from that, life has been stable. **Anthony** and I have worked hard to get to where we are now. Quitting **alcohol** was the best decision we ever made. It didn't come easy, but it was necessary. We no longer fight the way we used to. We're no longer drowning in the chaos that once ruled our lives. Instead, we've found a kind of peace that neither of us thought was possible.

But today, as I sit here writing, it's **October 5th**—the anniversary of my **biological father's death**. I can't help but feel like things have come full circle. The past still haunts me, but I've learned how to live with it. My father found me through an **ancestry DNA website**. We connected for a while, but it was always **strained**. I was angry at him, and I didn't know how to let that go.

He told me he hadn't been the one to sign me away when I was two years old. He claimed it had been his **brother**, who had the same name—**Johnny Clifton Robinson**. I wanted to believe him, but the documents said otherwise. His name was right there on the papers, clear as day. But I held onto his story because I wanted to believe that he hadn't abandoned me.

Then, two days before my **35th birthday**, he died. He passed away from **heart complications** and **dementia**, and I was left with nothing but unanswered questions. When I read his obituary, I found out the truth—it had been him who signed me away. He had lied to me, and now, I'll never get the answers I wanted.

That's something that still stays with me. The last thing he told me was a **lie**, and now he's gone. I regret not being kinder to him, not giving him more of a chance. But that's life, isn't it? Sometimes the things we want to forget are the things we need to confront, and sometimes the things we hold onto are better left buried.

I fear that one day **Caleb** will do the same to me. That he'll grow up, find out his own version of the truth, and resent me for it. I worry that he'll carry the same anger I had toward my father, and that this **cycle** will continue until someone has the strength to **break it**.

But for now, **Anthony** and I are doing the best we can. **Anthony** has been my rock through all of this. Living with someone as **unstable** and **broken** as I've been isn't easy. I have **bipolar disorder**, manic de-

pression, and a lifetime of trauma that seeps into everything I do. But Anthony is patient. He's the most patient man I've ever known, and probably the **first and only person** in my life who has ever loved me the right way.

He's my everything, and I love him more deeply than I've ever loved anyone. Together, we've created a life that is finally **stable**. We've built something that isn't perfect, but it's ours. It's the life we fought for, and it's the life we deserve.

CHAPTER 29

One Dollar Over a Hundred Pennies

Keeping the bond between us strong after all these years hasn't been easy. There were times when I wanted to give up, just as I'm sure there were times when **Anthony** did, too. But we didn't. We held on, even when it felt like the world was against us. We've faced more than our fair share of **demons** together—demons that could have easily torn us apart if we'd let them. But somehow, we came out on the other side.

One of the biggest challenges we've faced together is the dynamic with **Anthony's family**. His parents and sister live right down the road from us. They bought houses nearby, and while that might seem ideal for some families, it's always been complicated for us. **I don't talk to his family**, and they don't talk to me. There's no relationship there, no visits, no friendly chats. **Anthony** goes over to their houses sometimes, and they mostly just **talk and text**. But for me, they're not part of my life.

It's a strange feeling, being **married** to someone whose family hates you. But I've made peace with it. I've been through enough in my life to know that not everyone will like you, and that's okay. I'm not here to please people who don't matter. **Anthony** is the only person on this planet that I talk to. And while some people might see that as **unhealthy**, I see it as **freedom**. I've been through the wringer when it comes to relationships—family, friends, and everything in between. The more people I had in my life, the more I drank, the more I was **taken advantage of**, and the more I got hurt.

Cutting out the excess was the best decision I ever made. I don't need a large circle of friends or family to feel fulfilled. I'd rather have **one dollar** than a **hundred pennies**. For me, after all I've been through, that's enough. More than enough, actually.

Anthony filters out the bullshit, and he cuts straight to the point. He's the one person I trust. The one person I love. **My person.** I don't need the noise that comes with having too many people around. I don't need the drama, the misunderstandings, or the betrayals. I've had enough of that for a lifetime.

Being with **Anthony** has taught me so much—how to **love**, how to **trust**, and most importantly, how to be **kind**. He's shown me that I don't have to be angry all the time. That I don't have to be **mean** to protect myself. That I don't have to drink to be happy.

I've supported him in his weak times, just as he's supported me in mine. And together, we've done something I never thought possible: **we quit drinking**. We stopped drowning ourselves in **alcohol** and **pain**, and instead, we faced our problems head-on. The abuse, the trauma, the chaos—it's all still there, but it doesn't define us anymore.

What defines us now is **love**, **resilience**, and the **life we've built** together. A life that we've fought for. A life that is finally free of the toxic cycles we both came from. We've learned how to breathe, how to be **happy** without the constant stress of the past weighing us down.

Our home, filled with our **dogs**, is our sanctuary. Each dog, in their own way, has played a part in our healing. They remind us every day of the **unconditional love** we deserve. When I wake up to a pile of them cuddling around me, their little bodies pressed against mine, I'm reminded that this is the life I've earned. The life we've earned together.

The peace we have now didn't come easily. It's something we still work at. But we've built something **beautiful**—something that I never thought I could have. Anthony has taught me that I can let my guard down. That I can trust someone to love me without fear of betrayal. He's the only person who has ever loved me like this—the real way.

Looking back, I can see how much we've grown. From the darkness of our early years, filled with **fights** and **addiction**, to the **light** we've found now, where we can finally see a future together that isn't clouded by trauma or fear. We've **survived**. We've fought. And now, we're finally in a place where we can be happy, where we can **breathe**.

Anthony, our **dogs**, and this life we've created—they are my everything. They're all I need. The rest of the world can go on without me because, for the first time, I've found my place. My person. My peace.

CHAPTER 30

A Future Built on Truth

Looking forward, I have clear goals. Goals that, for the first time in my life, feel attainable. There's no more chaos, no more uncertainty. Just a path forward—a path I'm ready to walk with **Anthony** and the life we've built together.

One of my biggest goals is to **support Anthony** in his own dreams. He's not just my husband—he's an incredibly talented writer, and his vision for the **Patchwork Tales**, a children's book series, is something I believe in completely. I want to be there for him the way he's always been there for me. He has the creativity, the heart, and the ability to reach kids in a way that I could never do. My goal is to help him succeed, to give him the same unwavering support that he's always given me.

As for myself, I'll always stay on **Fiverr**. My psychic readings are more than just a career—they're a calling. They've given me a platform to connect with people, to help them navigate their own struggles, and to build something meaningful. I've built an empire on that platform, and I intend to keep growing it. I'll keep writing books under my professional name, expanding that side of my career, because it's something I'm deeply proud of. But there's more to my story than just that.

I want the world to hear **my story**. That's what this book is about. It's my truth, my life, and I'm putting it out there for people who might be on a similar path. I want this book to reach those who feel lost, broken, or like they'll never be able to escape their past. I want them to see that it's possible to change. It's possible to survive, to heal, and to create a life worth living—even if that life looks different from what society tells you it should be.

Sometimes it's okay to be alone. Sometimes having eight dogs is the best thing for your mental health. And sometimes, just because you weren't a good person in the past, doesn't mean you can't become one now. That's the message I want this book to send. I want people to know that their past doesn't define them. That they have the power to write their own future, no matter how dark their history might be.

That's why I wrote my song, **"I Won't Break,"** to go along with this book. It's more than just a track—it's an anthem of survival. I know it can help people who are in situations like mine. People who have been beaten down, written off, and left behind. It's a message of hope, of strength, and of refusing to be crushed by the weight of the past.

And then there's **Caleb**. I want nothing more than for him to have a **good life**. To be **successful** and **happy**, whatever that looks like for him. I know that someday, he might come looking for the truth. And when that day comes, I hope he doesn't hate me the way I hated my own father. I've written this book, in part, to get my truth out there, so that if Caleb ever finds it, he'll understand my side of the story.

I want him to know that I loved him—that I never stopped loving him. But I also know that it's his choice, and I respect that. He's an adult now, and I won't force myself into his life. I just hope that if he ever wants to know me, he'll find a way to reach out.

Writing this book hasn't been easy. **There's a lot I left out.** There are darker things I've endured, things I've never said out loud and probably never will. Some memories are just too painful, too raw, to ever share publicly. These are things only **Anthony** and I know. Things that will remain between us and the people who did them. But even though I've left those details out, what I've written here is the truth. Nothing has been fabricated or exaggerated. This is my life, laid bare for the world to see.

As I sit here writing this, I'm **turning 38 years old** in just two days, on **October 7th**. And for the first time in my life, I feel at peace. My goals for the future are simple: to remain **happy**, to remain **secure**, to remain **alcohol-free**, and to continue taking care of **Anthony** and our dogs the best I can.

I want to stay out of trouble. To keep living this life we've built without the weight of the past dragging me down. And most importantly, I want to continue learning how to **love**. That's been the hardest lesson of all—learning to love and to allow myself to be loved in return.

Anthony has taught me that not everyone is going to hurt me. That not everyone is out to take advantage of me or abandon me. He's shown me that love doesn't have to come with pain. And that's the lesson I'll carry with me into the next chapter of my life.

This book, **"I Won't Break,"** is a declaration of who I am and who I refuse to be. It's a testament to my **survival**, to my growth, and to the life I'm still building. **The story isn't finished**—not by a long shot. But this is where it stands today, and I'm proud of what I've accomplished.

The future is mine. And I won't break.

Final Reflections: Sink or Swim

I don't want anyone to feel sorry for me. I'm not a victim. Sure, I used to play that card—I used to think the world owed me everything. I'd been through hell, and I figured the Universe should pay me back for all the pain I'd endured. That mindset? It's what got me in trouble time and time again. But if there's one thing I've learned through all of this, it's that **the world doesn't owe you anything**.

You can either **sink or swim**, and I sank more times than I can count. There were moments when I was so far under, I didn't think I'd ever come back up. I tried to end it more than once. I thought there was no way out of the pain. But the **Universe**—or whatever force is out there—must have had some kind of purpose for me, because I'm still here. And now, looking back, I'm glad none of those attempts went through.

Everything that's happened to me, all the trauma, the abuse, the mistakes, the heartbreak—it all had a **purpose**. It's shaped me into the person I am today. It's brought me to **Anthony**, it's taught me how to love, how to survive, and how to write this book. I know now that every single experience, no matter how dark, happened for a reason.

And if I can get through it, **so can you**.

That's my message. Now that you know my story, I hope you see that it's possible to survive—even when it feels like the world is against you. Even when it feels like there's no way out. Don't let yourself get stuck in the cycle of **hate**. Don't let the trauma define you, no matter how heavy it feels.

Learn to **love yourself**. You deserve to be loved. You've **earned** it.

Derrick Solano is an alternative rock artist, author, and survivor who has lived through the kind of trauma that breaks most people—but he refused to be broken. Abandoned at the age of two, Derrick was thrust into the foster care system where he faced years of abuse, rejection, and betrayal. Adopted into a family that stripped him of his identity and manipulated him out of fatherhood, Derrick battled addiction, fought through mental health struggles, and endured unimaginable loss.

Through it all, Derrick found his salvation in music and writing. His raw, unfiltered art speaks to the depths of pain, survival, and the power of resilience. Derrick's debut single *I Won't Break* and his memoir of the same title tell a story of defiance in the face of every hardship life has thrown at him. His journey resonates with anyone who has ever felt lost, broken, or discarded by the world.

Derrick currently lives with his husband, Anthony, and their beloved dogs. After a lifetime of fighting to reclaim his own story, Derrick is now using his voice to inspire others who have been told they are not enough. His work is a testament to the strength it takes to survive and the refusal to let the world break him.